Ronald F. Connolly, Ed.D.   Christopher J. Utecht, M.S.

A GUIDE TO WRITING
QUALITY POLICE REPORTS

Kendall Hunt
publishing company

Cover image ©Shutterstock, Inc.

www.kendallhunt.com
Send all inquiries to:
4050 Westmark Drive
Dubuque, IA 52004-1840

Copyright © 2018 by Kendall Hunt Publishing Company

ISBN 978-1-5249-5810-7

Published in the United States of America

CONTENTS

ACKNOWLEDGEMENTS AND DEDICATION

I would like to offer my heartfelt gratitude to the Cities of Milwaukee and Appleton Police Departments for providing me with the professional experience that is incumbent of those wishing to influence future generations to be quality professionals. Further, I extend sincere gratitude to the academic institutions from which I obtained my own education and the colleges and university that have allowed my contribution to the education of others. I thank my good friend and co-author, Christopher Utecht, for his intellectual engagement and drive that were instrumental in the motivation to see this project through. Finally, I thank my family for their patience and encouragement during the demanding process of developing this publication.

To Caroline and Cameron, being your father has been my greatest achievement and I admire you as the quality individuals that you have become. You are both my inspiration and I dedicate this work to you!

—Ron Connolly

My thanks and praise go to my wife Erica, who should be granted an honorary PhD in Criminal Justice after all of the proofreading she's done for me throughout the years. Harvey, Arlene, Randy and Sandy; Adeline, Otto, Helen and Hazel; Chiefs Arleigh Porter and Dan Trelka; and my co-author Ron Connolly: thank you all for your support, encouragement, and guidance throughout the years.

—Christopher Utecht

Ron Connolly, Ed.D

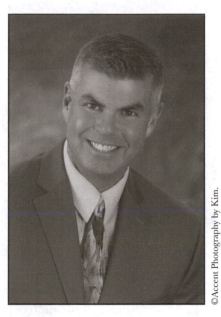

©Accent Photography by Kim.

Dr. Ron Connolly began his career path with the Milwaukee Police Department, as a Police Aide and later, as a decorated Police Officer. In 1990, he sought to reach beyond his community to serve as a Chief Warrant Officer and Aviator in the United States Army. His return from active duty offered an opportunity with the Appleton Police Department, where he worked, initially as a Patrol Officer and later, as a Senior Sergeant, entrusted with gang, narcotics and criminal intelligence Investigations. In 1998, he was awarded the honor of being the Appleton Police Department Officer of the Year and, in 2002, he earned the Outagamie County District Attorney's Best Badge Award. Life-long learning has always been a priority for Ron. Early on, he graduated with a Bachelor's Degree in Criminal Justice from Mount Senario College, but felt compelled to discover more about the role of leaders in human interaction. Ron is an alumnus of Marian University, where he obtained his Master of Science Degree in Organizational Leadership and Quality. That experience inspired him to the attainment of an Educational Doctorate in Leadership, for the Advancement of Learning and Service from Cardinal Stritch University. With a focus on helping future generations to strive for excellence, he began teaching as an adjunct instructor at Fox Valley Technical College. In 2004, he transitioned to teaching full-time at Northcentral Technical College, in Wausau, WI. By 2009, Dr. Connolly accepted the opportunity to teach at Northeast Wisconsin Technical College, in Green Bay, WI, as a Criminal Justice Instructor, specializing in ethics and leadership training. Since 2016, Dr. Connolly has served as Associate Professor of Criminal Justice at Marian University. For nearly two decades, he has been an Academy Instructor/Master Instructor, an Associate Degree educator, and, most recently, an undergraduate and graduate degree professor. In addition to being a tactical instructor, Ron has focused on disciplines such as Constitutional and criminal law, crisis intervention, traffic law enforcement and incident investigation and, since 1999, has been teaching police report writing. His extra-curricular endeavors include presentations such as, "The Bystander Effect," sponsored by the Marian University Social Justice Committee; "Becoming a 'Superhero' in the Workplace," for Women's Specialty Care Health Clinic; "Building Mindful Relationships," for Bellin Health; "Customer-focused Leadership," for the Radisson Paper Valley Hotel Security Department; and a statewide "Ethics Instructor Update Series," for the Wisconsin Department of Justice. Dr. Connolly is also a former Director on the Law Enforcement Training Officer's Association—Board of Directors.

Courtesy Christopher Utecht.

Christopher Utecht, MS

Christopher Utecht, MS, has served as a law enforcement officer in Wisconsin for 15-years, working for the UW-Milwaukee, Washington Island, and Sturgeon Bay Police Departments as an officer before attaining the rank of Chief with the Dover Water Patrol. In addition to the duties incumbent on a Chief, during his career Chris has worked in a variety of police roles, including patrol officer, tactical team member, marine officer, and field-trainer. He began his move into academia by teaching as adjunct faculty at Northeast Wisconsin Technical College in Green Bay, WI. Chris is currently a full time Associate Professor in the Criminal Justice Department at the College of Lake County in Grayslake, IL. He is a regular presenter at regional and national conferences, including the Academy of Criminal Justice Sciences (ACJS) Annual Meeting. Chris is also the Secretary-Treasurer of the ACJS Community College section. His writing appears in the journal Multicultural Perspectives. He holds a Master of Science degree in Criminal Justice from the University of Cincinnati, and is currently pursuing a Master of Arts in Applied Sociology at the University of Alabama at Birmingham. In his free time he enjoys fishing and travelling with his family, especially in the Florida Keys.

INTRODUCTION

For those entering a career in policing, the idea of quality report writing may not necessarily emerge as a priority. However, new officers find out in short order that skilled written communication is the foundation of effective service to the community. Due to its recognized importance to the professional life of officers, police report writing has a long history in police education. A quick check of Amazon.com yields over 100 results for the search term "police report writing." In consideration of this publication as a tool for building police report writing skills, it's natural to ask, "Why this book? What on earth could possibly be new under the sun?" While it's true that the fundamentals of police report writing remain consistent, recent events have lent themselves to the consideration of new elements that must be incorporated into the training involved in police report writing. Although this manual does not seek to deviate from the fundamentals, there are subtle nuances that should be added to the traditional curriculum to enhance the capabilities of quality report writing.

Traditionally police reports begin with a paragraph that explains who the originator of the report is, how and when that person became aware of the subject of the report, and the location of the incident being documented. The next paragraph begins with the officer's arrival at the scene and a documentation of the various facets of the investigation of the matter. Subsequent paragraphs present details related to the event, incident, or investigation. The final paragraph of the report generally documents resolution of the incident or areas of consideration for further action. We acknowledge that these are essential components of police report writing and have no desire to imply that their importance should be diminished. However, contemporary occurrences, particularly involving critical incidents such as officer-involved shootings (from Ferguson, Missouri [2014] to Baton Rouge, Louisiana [2016] and unfortunately many more) have shed light on the necessity to document the officer's thought process and perceptions during the span between being made initially aware of a situation and the arrival on the scene, as well as throughout the entire investigation. Quite often, such thoughts and perceptions do not surface until the case reaches the scrutiny of the legal system, enabling the erosion of recall due to the passage of time and opening the door for allegations of breaches of integrity. It is our contention that if these particulars were documented in the police report, it would lend more credibility to the officer in court and increase the apparent transparency of the police organization and the criminal justice system. It also enables analysis of the situation from a more humanistic perspective rather than simply as an official response.

The reader may also note that this publication differs from many of its contemporaries in that it offers a combination of fundamentals of report writing and hands-on exercises. The book is formatted to appeal to the interactive learning styles of many police officers. The information portion of this book is front-loaded, with the bulk of the book geared toward skill-building and practical exercises. It is our goal that by using this book, you will become a better report writer and will be able to refresh and sustain those skills throughout your career. By doing so, you will enable yourself to succeed professionally and simultaneously increase public safety throughout your community.

While this book seeks to instruct in a manner suitable for all agencies, students are cautioned to consult their supervisor and agency policies for the particulars of how their agency wants report writing done. They should also consult with their local prosecutor, as that person will ultimately be the one using the report as the foundation for any criminal complaint and prosecution.

PART I

FUNDAMENTALS OF POLICE REPORT WRITING

PRIMARY COLLISION FACTOR
LIST NUMBER (#) OF PARTY AT FAULT

A   VC SECTION VIOLATED.

B   OTHER IMPROPER DRIVING.

C   OTHER THAN DRIVER*

D   UNKNOWN*

CHAPTER 1

THE PURPOSE OF POLICE REPORTS

COMPETENCY 1: Describe the purpose of police reports.

LEARNING OBJECTIVE 1: Identify various users/readers of police reports.

When it comes to police reports, the purpose is as varied as the types of incidents. For example, consider a simple traffic crash report. For the individuals involved in the crash, it is a record of what happened. For an insurance adjuster, the same report may be used to assess liability. A city planner may use the report to provide data for justification of the improvement of traffic controls. For the police administration, it may be an indicator that a particular area is in need of additional patrol. And that is just for a simple traffic crash report. Consider the wide range of potential users for the information contained in a felony arrest report. So, how does someone arrive at a universal definition of a police report?

With regard to as many applications of police reports as possible, we have chosen to identify the purpose to be: *to communicate facts to others in such a manner that they understand what occurred without having been a witness to the occurrence.* Consider the above example. What do the individuals involved in the crash, the insurance adjuster, the police administration, and the city planner all have in common? They simply want to know what happened and, in most cases were not present to observe, first-hand, the information being documented within the report. This is one of the core principles of police report writing, that the officer is creating a record of the occurrence.

Recall, from the history of policing, why our version of policing was created. Police were commissioned to be neutral, third-party mediators/arbitrators of disputes. They were commissioned to decide matters without having an interest in the matter themselves. This is why police reports can be so powerful. They represent a disinterested third-party account set down as the permanent and official record.

"The purpose of police reports is to communicate the facts to others in such a manner that they understand what occurred without having been a witness to the occurrence."

WHO READS POLICE REPORTS?

YOU DO!

Perhaps the most important person to read your report is you, the reporting officer. Writing a report is your opportunity to create a permanent record of what you have observed in a given situation or what you have uncovered during an investigation. It is a way for you to document your methods and your timeline. In some ways, report writing is like leaving a note on your kitchen counter to remind you of something. In this case, though, the reminder is for your future self, reminding you about the details of a case. In court, you will be called upon to testify about the events of an incident. Your report is the record of that incident and what you did. Thorough writing can take a lot of pressure off of you in court, because you will be able to more easily remember the details of a case if you have a detailed report.

Report writing is also a way for you to examine your work and determine what work yet needs to be done, both in the case and in your career. Throughout history, writing has been used for introspection and exploration of one's self. Police report writing is no different. When writing a report, you will invariably uncover aspects of the incident that you missed or information that you forgot to obtain. These are not only potential items to follow up on, but they are also points for consideration moving forward. Introspection is a powerful tool for learning throughout the career of a police officer. Report writing provides a chance for you to examine your missteps and a prompt for self-improvement.

Your Agency (Supervisors and Administration)

Consider the usefulness that a single, well-written report holds. It can help a supervisor assess the quality of work being generated from a subordinate while also shedding light on how well a police department is addressing a particular issue. The same report provides guidance for investigators involved in an ongoing case, or refreshing an officer's memory prior to taking the stand in court. Agency revenues, approval for expansion of services, and development of special initiatives often hinge on data derived from officer reports. If you stop to think about it, any given police report represents a "multi-tool" frequently and effectively used at all levels of a police agency.

The Courts: Judges, Prosecutors, Defense, Juries, Witnesses

As noted, police are expected to be neutral fact finders. Consider also that your report is an official record. For both of these reasons, and more, you will be expected to testify in court from time to time. Your report is an integral part of the court process. The prosecutor uses it to determine the type and amount of charges to be filed in a criminal complaint. Defense attorneys use it to see the government's side of the story so they can prepare their client's defense. Judges see your report writing skills when you author a search warrant affidavit. Juries use your report when deliberating a verdict. Witnesses can obtain your report through an open records request to refresh their memories about an incident.

Furthermore, all of these individuals associated with the court process will be using your report to determine your level of professionalism. Writing a thorough report helps to show that an officer is professional and squared away. Consider the amount of confidence a prosecutor will have in presenting his or her case if the main witness, a police officer, seems squared away and professional from their writing. The flipside of this is that assembling a poorly written report can give others the opinion that you are unprofessional, unprepared, or careless. Consider the amount of confidence a defense attorney will have in defending a client if the prosecution's main witness, a police officer, seems sloppy or lackadaisical from their writing. Clearly, if you are going to have to write a report, it should be complete, detailed, and exacting in order to present the most professional picture possible.

Other Governmental Agencies and Community Resources

There are times when officers, assigned singly to their patrol areas, may be perceived as being alone in carrying out their duties. On the surface, that appearance may seem valid, but the reality is, in addition to the support and assistance of other officers, supervisors, and administrators, each officer has an arsenal of additional governmental agencies and community resources to tap into. Problem solving that involves cooperation and coordination between the police and other available resources occurs on a regular basis. To ensure that all of the contributors to a solution share a common understanding of the problem to be solved, the police report is in place to keep them informed. Agencies such as the Department of Transportation or the Department of Natural Resources will rely on officer reports to enhance their own investigations, or assist in the efforts of other officials. Community resources such as homeless shelters, food pantries, at-risk youth diversionary organizations, etc., may rely on police reports to justify their efforts, or even their very existence. State, county, and municipal planners, licensing bodies, and housing authorities frequently review officer reports to gain perspective on matters that they are considering for approval or denial (liquor licenses, bartending licenses, solicitation permits, housing assistance, etc.).

Media

Two of the greatest protections guaranteed in the U.S. Constitution are the First Amendment rights to freedom of speech and freedom of the press. Those very rights empower the media (television, radio, newspapers, internet, and electronic communication) to openly report information that ranges from public service announcements to the sensational. For the price of an open-records fee, the media has access to public records and, more specifically, police reports. Much praise is due the media in cases of reporting that resulted in the location of a missing person, apprehension of a known fugitive, or the outreach of the community to a person in need. However, caution must be taken to ensure that the confidentiality of information related to children, victims, informants, etc., is maintained. In addition, it is important to recognize that there are times when the media may seek more information from officers than what they are entitled to share.

Special Interest Groups

Special interest groups such as Black Lives Matter or the Southern Poverty Law Center are sometimes seen as adversaries by the police. Their agenda can seem to run contrary to that of the police or can at least cause the police a measure of frustration. Consider the mission of special interest groups: to improve the lives of whatever group they represent. Generally these are noble causes; however, the police, as the most visible and most accessible government actors, often run afoul of these groups. These groups will also be interested in your reports. Thorough report writing can help to stimulate understanding, improve transparency, and reduce tension. Slipshod or careless report writing can lead to increased tension, as well as the appearance that the police have something to hide.

Insurance Companies

Insurance companies are concerned with liability and risk. They use police reports to determine who is liable in a given situation and how much to pay out based on that level of liability. Insurance companies also use police reports to calculate risk, which is a key determinant in insurance policy rates. Be aware that insurance companies are motivated by mitigating their degree of liability rather than seeking an objective account of an occurrence. Police reports may be supplemented to reflect new, factual discoveries, but reports should never be altered to conform to a scenario that best suits an insurance company. A supplemental report may be filed for the purpose of documenting additional facts which may or may not support the position of an insurance company.

Citizens (Victims, Suspects, Property Owners, Witnesses, Curious People, Basically Anyone Who is Authorized to Access Public Records)

Generally, anyone who is authorized to access public records can request a copy of a police report. This could truly be any interested party, from a property owner who was the victim of vandalism, to a nosy neighbor who wants to know what was going on up the street. Understand that your report is the official record of what happened in an incident. All of the details included in your report, including any opinions offered or extraneous information, are available to the public for the cost of an open records request. While this should not make a police officer wary about completing a detailed report, officers are cautioned to maintain a neutral tone as well as to be concise, including only relevant information in their reports. The use of opinions should be limited, and when used should be qualified as such, and supported by facts—for instance, an officer's opinion of impairment by alcohol of a subject who has failed field sobriety testing.

CONCLUSION

To this point, we have discussed the various purposes associated with police reports and identified some of the people with an interest in reading them. The types of police reports consistently used from agency to agency are almost as numerous as the types of people with an interest in reading them. In the next chapter, we will be examining a variety of reports that an officer can expect to encounter throughout a career.

CHAPTER 2

TYPES OF REPORTS

COMPETENCY 2: Differentiate reports based on type and purpose.

LEARNING OBJECTIVE 1: Describe various types of reports.
LEARNING OBJECTIVE 2: Contrast structural components of various types of reports.

Just as there are a variety of purposes for police reports, there are a range of report types. The type of report needed for an incident will generally be determined by the purpose of the report. Consider the example used in Chapter 1: a simple traffic crash. Obviously this type of incident will probably result in the completion of a *traffic crash report*. However, based on the circumstances, it may require more reports than just that report. If there is serious property damage, or an injury, the reporting officer will probably need to complete an *incident report*. If the subject is intoxicated, in addition to the *traffic crash report* and *incident report*, the officer will likely have to complete an *arrest report*, in addition to completing some *traffic citations*. After arresting the subject for operating while intoxicated, the officer will probably collect evidence, such as an evidentiary breath or blood sample, which will make an *evidence report* necessary. Finally, if the intoxicated motorist ends up fighting with the officer, a *use of force report* will also be needed. All of this from a "simple" traffic crash. This chapter provides an overview of the most common reports written by police officers in order to help you start the process of considering what information you will need to collect in any incident you respond to.

INCIDENT REPORT

A variety of reports are often included in the category of "incident report." Such reports range from reports of violation of criminal law to civil disputes, to reports of missing persons, suspicious persons, or even officer-supervised exchanges of property. An incident report, in part or full narrative format, simply documents the details of a specific occurrence as reported to, or observed by, the police.

ARREST REPORT

An arrest report documents the apprehension of a criminal violator. It includes the crime with which the arrestee is charged, the date, time and location of the arrest, and the name and agency of the arresting officer. Generally it also includes information pertaining to the location to which the arrestee was transported and confined.

FIELD INTERVIEW/CITIZEN CONTACT

Terry Stop

(also known as an "Investigative Detention" or "Stop and Frisk") the authority to conduct an investigative detention and frisk of a criminal suspect. Its purpose is to conduct a brief investigation to confirm or deny that the suspect is involved in criminal activity (Argiriou, n.d.).

A field interview/citizen contact report is similar to an incident report. Field interviews are just what the name implies: interviews of individuals on the street. These can arise when an officer observes what he or she considers to be suspicious behavior and conducts a **Terry Stop.** If the circumstance ultimately turns out to be noncriminal, the officer releases the subject from the scene. However, the officer must complete a report to place the individual at a certain location at a certain time, in the event that new information comes to light about the incident and the department needs to interview the subject again.

Citizen contacts are simply interactions officers have with individuals on the street. An example would be if a shopkeeper wanted to report that juveniles were skateboarding in the downtown area in violation of city ordinances, but the juveniles were nowhere to be found at the time of report. Another example is when an officer is dispatched to a car with a flat tire and the officer stands by while the subject changes the tire. Both types of incidents are noncriminal in nature but still involve the police and require police to record what happened. In minor, nonserious cases like these, some departments use an attenuated report form, sometimes the size of a note card, for officers to document the incident for future reference. These forms can also be used to document advice or warnings given to individuals. Depending on the department, these reports could be called a citizen contact report, a field interview (FI) card, or a miscellaneous report form.

EVIDENCE COLLECTION REPORT

An evidence collection report offers a detailed description of evidence collected in relation to a specific incident. The report documents the date, time, and location of where the evidence was recovered, the name of the person who recovered it, and the location in which the evidence is being inventoried and stored.

MEMORANDUM / "IN THE MATTER OF" REPORT

A memorandum, also known as a memo or a "In the matter of" report, is an intra-agency communication. In Latin the word *memorandum* means "to bring to mind." These types of reports are used to document happenings inside the department. A supervisor might ask that a memorandum be submitted when an officer damages a piece of equipment, such as backing into a pole with a squad. Their purpose is to memorialize, or record, the facts of an incident for future reference.

SUPPLEMENTAL REPORT

A supplemental report is associated with an original report and is used to document additional factual information discovered at a date and time after the initial incident report was taken. Examples would be a new witness coming to light, discovery of additional property damage, or an officer completing a follow-up investigation.

TRAFFIC CRASH REPORT

Commonly called an "accident report," crash reports are documentation of vehicle collisions. These are one of the most common reports completed by police officers. These are usually form reports, with fields to be completed and boxes to be checked. They may also include a brief area for a narrative description of the crash, as well as an area for the officer to complete a diagram of the crash scene.

CITATION

A citation is a report of issuance of a municipal ordinance or traffic law to a violator. It contains several informational fields such as the identity of the violator, the violation, the date, time, and location of the violation, the penalty or forfeiture associated with the violation, and the court date and location (should the violation be contested). Also included in most citations is a narrative area in which the officer documents the circumstances leading up to the issuance of the citation.

PROBABLE CAUSE AFFIDAVIT

A probable cause affidavit is the constitutionally required statement supported by oath or affirmation that a judge evaluates prior to authorizing a warrant. In the case of an arrest warrant, a probable cause statement outlines that there is probable cause to believe that a specific person committed a specific crime. In the case of a search warrant, a probable cause statement outlines the officer's probable cause to believe that there is specific evidence of a certain crime at a specific location. Either of these will be completed by officers during the course of an investigation, but only after they have a quantity of evidence to believe a crime probably occurred.

USE OF FORCE

Police use of force is a considered a Fourth Amendment seizure. Any interference with a subject's liberty is considered a seizure and must be justified. Therefore, any time an officer uses force it must be justified and documented, whether the degree of force was applied during handcuffing, using their firearm, or any point in between. A use of force report will address the following items: the justification for using force (e.g., subject behaviors), the type/level of force used, justification for using that type/level of force, the person the police used force against, identification of the officers who used the force, and the outcome of the situation.

CONCLUSION

There are as many types of police reports as there are purposes for police report. Officers must be aware of the information they will need to gather for the type of report that they will have to write for a given incident. These officers must also bear in mind that they may have to write multiple types of reports for a single incident. At the beginning of your career, this will seem daunting; however, with experience, officers will come to recognize the multiplicity of report types needed while they are in the process of handling the incident on scene.

CHAPTER 3

PREPARATION

In any serious undertaking, you need to prepare yourself. If you have ever played sports, you know about the importance of fundamentals. For instance, without skills in dribbling, passing, and shooting, basketball would be a very hard game, indeed! The same is true in police report writing. To write a good police report, officers must know why they are writing the report (Chapter 1) and, based on this, the type of report they need to write (Chapter 2). In this chapter you will learn about the next fundamental skill of police report writing: note-taking. Note-taking is a process of writing down the various steps taken in an investigation and the information and evidence uncovered as part of that investigation. Good note-taking will also allow an officer to analyze the work performed to help him or her understand what needs to be done next, and what aspects of the case are suspicious or need further investigation.

INVESTIGATION/INFORMATION GATHERING

Note-taking

Human beings are capable of amazing things, but unfortunately they are not equipped with unlimited capacity for recall. For that reason, concise, accurate, and understandable note-taking is an essential element of any thorough investigation. Regardless of the type of incident (criminal, traffic, civil disturbance, etc.), appropriate note-taking serves as the foundation of the ability to accurately convey the circumstances of an occurrence to parties who were not present at the time of the event. Remember, if you complete an investigation of the highest quality, but are unable to accurately document the steps of your investigation, it will negate all of the hard work that you put into developing the case.

Field notes are brief notations concerning specific events that the officer encounters in the performance of his or her duties (WI DOJ, 2014). You will use these notes to document your on-scene observations, the people you spoke to, and what they had to say. This will help you to remember such details for your report, as well as to help you eliminate duplication of efforts by enhancing your ability to communicate who has already been interviewed and who still needs to be interviewed.

Tools of Note-taking

In general, field notes are recorded in a duty notebook. Such notebooks should be small enough in size to fit in a back pocket, cargo pocket, or shirt breast pocket. It should be large enough to fit comfortably in the user's hand, and be sturdy enough to write in without the support of a desk or other sort of platform. When selecting your notebook, take into consideration that you will usually be writing in it while standing, supporting the notebook with your hand only. Also consider your officer safety in this process: you do not want a notebook that is so large that it will obstruct your view while taking notes. Check your agency policy to determine if your department requires a certain type of notebook. If not, select a notebook based on the above considerations.

A further consideration: writing implements. Consider the climate in which you will be working. Pens have a tendency to freeze up in cold weather. Ink has a tendency to run when it gets wet in the rain. Furthermore, pens have a tendency not to write on wet paper. For all these reasons, it is important to carry a variety of different writing implements, to include a standard pen, a small permanent marker, and a pencil to facilitate note-taking in various weather conditions.

Another consideration in note-taking is the public records laws in your state. As a government employee, your notes may be considered a public record, and you may be required to make them available for inspection and/or discovery at trial. You may also be required to maintain your notes for a period of time dictated by state statute or department policy. It is important to be aware of these requirements and to avoid writing untoward comments in your notes or irrelevant information in your notebook (e.g., your kids' basketball schedules).

Note-taking Process

Noteworthy information often materializes at the moment that an officer is dispatched to an incident, witnesses an occurrence, or is made aware of an event through any other means. At that point, the officer should be concerned with a number of approach considerations: "What direction should I approach from? Will I need assistance at the scene? Is it necessary to have the fire department or rescue respond as well?" Many times, decisions that are made within seconds, during a response, will be scrutinized in extensive detail by reviewers at various points in the future.

Just as important as approach considerations, initial observations of the scene upon the officer's arrival are essential to note. Scene assessment will have a direct bearing on a responding officer's subsequent actions. To develop a thorough report, notes should reflect the initial observations of the officer, his or her subsequent reaction, and the reasoning behind it. These observations will also be scrutinized in extensive detail by reviewers.

To enable such reviewers to understand reasons behind decisive action, it is often important for the officer to explain his or her thought process during the development of approach considerations through initial observations. Brief notes relating to thoughts and actions during incident response may be helpful in preserving and relating the mindset of the officer at the time, and the reasoning behind the action of the moment. For instance, an officer responding to a burglary call arrives on scene and observes a subject matching the dispatched description in front of the residence. The officer exits the squad car, draws a weapon, and takes the subject into custody. Later it is determined that the subject in custody was simply a bystander in the wrong place at the wrong time. When the subject makes a complaint with the department about the officer, or files a lawsuit against the department alleging a violation of civil rights, it will be critically important to the officer and the department that the officer is able to articulate his or her thought process behind taking the subject into custody. This thought process will determine the reasonableness of the officer's actions and if such actions were taken in good faith.

Once on scene, an officer will invariably have to gather information from others, such as victims, witnesses, and complainants. A key component of accurate note-taking is active listening. Before taking out your notepad, listen to what you are hearing from the people on scene, whether the statement is made spontaneously or is the result of questioning by the officer.

When interviewing people, be sure to listen actively. Hear their story out, evaluate their statement, and ask clarifying questions. Then begin your process of taking field notes about their statement. Oftentimes, officers in the field are subjected to perceived time pressures to get through their calls as quickly as possible. But as the old saying goes, haste makes waste. No matter how quickly you are able to process through your calls, if you are not collecting complete and accurate information, you are potentially handicapping the future prospects of closing the case for yourself or any other investigating officers. Your investigations are done on your time; you are in charge of your scene and the information that arises from your investigation. Generally, it will be you, not your supervisor or peers, who is conducting your investigation. Be sure to take the time to actively listen and get complete information in your field notes.

Types of Information

During any investigation, consider three types of information: perishable, semi-perishable, and permanent. Perishable information requires immediate collection and documentation because it is subject to rapid deterioration or change. For example, latent prints, accident scene debris, blood stains, fruits of criminal activity, and electronic information are all subject to potential removal, alteration, or destruction either through either intentional or unintentional action, inadvertent contact, or act of nature.

Semi-perishable information has a limited shelf-life. This type of information will not disappear immediately or be subject to immediate change. However, it is likely to change or disappear over a relatively short period of time. Semi-perishable information, though not as fleeting as perishable information, is not permanent and thus requires quick action. Examples of this type of information are tire skid marks, ruts, and impressions, or certain types of damage to property such as graffiti, tool marks, and paint transfer. Like perishable information, it is critically important that semi-perishable information be documented quickly and accurately so that it is able to be used in a case.

Permanent information is comprised of evidence or circumstances that are not likely to change within a short period of time. Examples would include social security numbers, driver's license numbers, and locations of physical features such as sewer grates, buildings, or land characteristics.

Photographs and Video

Photographs and video are often helpful tools in preparing to write reports and can significantly assist in the recording of accurate notes; however, there is a caution. Officers cannot exclusively rely on them as the basis for reports. As they are two-dimensional media, perspective is difficult to distinguish without the inclusion of an associated scale of measurement. Light, shading, and physical dimension can be skewed by the lens and the perspective of the camera. Additionally, it is important that a photo log is maintained to document what each of the photographs displays.

Good note-taking is still critical, even when photographs and video are available. Photographs are only as good as the photographer. If the person taking the photographs did a poor job of documenting the scene, it places an even heavier emphasis on the quality of your note-taking. Also, as Murphy's law tells us, whatever can go wrong, will go wrong. Film (if still in use) can sometimes not develop, digital media (of all types) can be corrupted, and video can malfunction. Also, due to the dynamic nature of police encounters, video has a tendency to **not** capture the most important aspects of a situation. The tendency for photography and video to malfunction when it is needed most further emphasizes the need for high-quality note-taking.

Electronically Assisted Measurement Devices

Electronically assisted measurement devices may also be helpful implements in gathering investigative information and often are less cumbersome to handle than conventional measurement tools. For example, lasers may be used to determine range in a matter of seconds and, in many cases, may only require one person to gather such information. Conversely, measuring a crime scene through the use of a tape measure often requires two people and is limited by the length of the measuring tape. Additionally, the tape is cumbersome to work with, is subject to inaccuracies when exposed to elements (such as the wind), and gathers dirt. A three-dimensional forensic scanner can be used to completely diagram a crime scene in short order, however, it is not impervious to mechanical or electronic failure. Therefore, field notes should always be taken. Consider that while the depiction created by a three-dimensional forensic scanner is very accurate, it is meaningless without an officer's description of what the image details. As such, field notes are critically important, in order to provide the most complete depiction of the crime scene, even when these measuring devices are used.

Consistency in Note-taking

One of the keys to quality note-taking is developing a consistent method for obtaining data. This will help officers ensure they are obtaining the data necessary for a quality report. In terms of consistency in recording the identifying information of persons or automobiles, it is critical that the note-taker establishes a template for gathering such information. To avoid gaps in identification, the note-taker should strictly adhere to an established template. Officers must develop a method that works for them and one that they are comfortable with. A suggested information gathering template (as follows) represents one version of such an implement.

Personal data:
Last Name, First Name, Middle Name or Initial, Race/Sex, Date of Birth
Street Address, City, State, Zipcode
Phone Numbers, with type documented (home, cell, etc.)

Example:
Public, John Q, W/M, 7/4/1976
123 Main Street, Dubuque, IA 52001
Home: 563-589-0000

Vehicle Data:
State of Registration, Plate Type (if known), Registration Plate Number or Vehicle Identification Number (VIN) if there is no Plate Number
Vehicle Color, Vehicle Year, Vehicle Make, Vehicle Model, Vehicle Body Type (e.g., 2-door, 4-door, coupe, sedan, station wagon, SUV, truck)

Example:
Wisconsin Automobile Plate ABC-123
Tan, 1997, Pontiac, Bonneville, 4-door

Certainly the investigator may collect information in an order he or she is comfortable doing. Regardless of template format, note-takers should use their established template in the same manner every time they engage in information gathering to avoid missing critical information.

PLANNING STRUCTURE OF THE REPORT

After the officer has completed the preliminary investigation, the work of composing the report begins. Composing the report should happen as soon as possible, so that the officer has the details fresh in mind, free from the interference of information from other cases. However, prior to writing, officers must consider why they are writing the report, what type of report needs to be written, and who they are writing the report for.

Why Is the Officer Writing the Report?

Official reports range in variety from informational, to investigatory, to documentational and each purpose requires its own unique format and type of information that must be included. For example, an accident report is comprised of an entirely different format than an inventory report. A criminal offense report bears little resemblance to an interdepartmental memorandum. Prior to composing your report, identify the purpose of the report and transcribe the content of your notes into the appropriate report format.

What Type of Report Needs to Be Written?

In consideration of the purpose of the report, officers must be sure to compose the type of report needed for the situation. In most cases, this should be fairly straightforward. A traffic crash clearly calls for a traffic crash report. A criminal violation, such as a burglary, calls for an offense report. But what about a traffic crash that results in the two drivers fighting—one of the drivers fights with the police, injures an officer, and gets sprayed with a chemical agent. Is that a traffic crash report, an offense report, an injury memorandum, or a use of force report? Based on agency policy, the answer may be "all of the above." Perhaps the reporting officer or officers will need to file all four of these types of reports. Each officer involved may need to file separate reports, especially if multiple officers used force. This step in the planning process is important to the officers writing reports for a number of reasons, including proper documentation, accountability, and the prospect of disciplinary action against officers for failing to complete required paperwork.

Who Is the Officer Writing the Report For?

This is the part of the planning process where the officer considers the intended audience for his or her report. Content of the report must be tailored to the level of understanding of the reader. For example, with regard to an interdepartmental memorandum, using terminology that is common place within the organization may be entirely acceptable and understood. However, an offence report, which may be utilized by a jury as part of the evidence, has to be written using language that anyone without specialized police training and experience could understand. Therefore, careful consideration should be given to ensure that what you are writing will be understood by your intended audience.

CONCLUSION

Adequate preparation is one of the keys to quality report writing. This chapter outlined the skills and tools needed for writing police reports. Principal to this preparation process is thorough note-taking. The skill of note-taking permeates all aspects of the policing profession. It allows officers to write good reports, track what steps they have taken in an investigation, and plan what they need to do next. The activities that follow allow you to practice those skills. In the next chapter, you will learn how to convert those notes to a quality police report narrative.

NOTE-TAKING ACTIVITY

For each individual listed below, place their personal information in the proper order on the lines provided. Information should be written as it would appear in your memo book (as instructed in class).

Example:
Carson, William T.
Black / Male (B/M), DOB: 07-13-88
2317 W. 92nd St. Vernon, WI 59646
(920) 847-9031

_____

_____

_____

_____

1433 Lawrence Circle, Pipe, WI 54936

Tanya V. Edwards

(414) 375-6280

White / Female (F/W)

DOB: 04-17-82

_____

_____

_____

_____

Black / Male (B/M)

(920) 869-2727

47 Tory Drive, Cedar Creek, WI 53219

Devon M. Kinnard

DOB: 10-13-74

_____

_____

_____

_____

DOB: 03-11-91

Wendy A. Belton

(715) 298-1623

Asian / Female (A/F)

5398 Morgan Ave., Darby, WI 58342

_____   Dennis H. Wilby

_____   1680 Tennyson Place, Trenton, WI 56772

_____   White / Male (W/M)

_____   DOB: 05-28-76

(608) 234-0803

_____   (262) 435-2382

_____   DOB: 11-09-96

_____   Hispanic / Female (H/F)

_____   7342 Ashland Center, Gilman, WI 51899

Salena A. Arnez

_____   3518 Cory Anne Way, Pittsville, WI 56992

_____   (920) 771-1880

_____   Asian / Female (A/F)

_____   DOB: 06-14-2003

Xai (nmi) Lee

_____   Black / Female (B/F)

_____   93 Concord Circle, Clayburn, WI 57321

_____   Roberta S. Klein

_____   (715) 527-1384

DOB: 01-12-59

_____

_____

_____

_____

Burton L. Jennings

Black / Male (B/M)

1414 Thomson Cove, Alberta, WI 52116

DOB: 04-21-84

(414) 964-1007

_____

_____

_____

_____

DOB: 12-18-76

Xiong Y. Vang

(715) 232-5026

7310 Oakwood Terrace, Cobb, WI 51218

Asian / Male (A/M)

_____

_____

_____

_____

809 N. 36th St., Dunford, WI 58707

DOB: 08-18-79

Chelsea R. Conroy

White / Female (W/F)

(414) 632-5619

_____

_____

_____

_____

White / Male (W/M)

(608) 246-0031

DOB: 09-03-62

7831 W. 114th Ave., Elmhurst, WI 53602

Trevor B. Adams

_____

_____

_____

_____

141 Morning Glory Dr., Danville, WI 57772

Hispanic / Male (H/M)

Salvatore V. Gomez

(262) 355-2226

DOB: 09-26-54

_____

_____

_____

_____

Black / Male (B/M)

Morton S. Pettigrew

(414) 684-5269

DOB: 02-24-96

75 14 W. Sunnyvale Ct., Wilton, WI 53412

_____

_____

_____

_____

DOB: 05-19-77

(920) 604-7301

Howard L. Cho

8799 E. Camden Way, Ogden, WI 57934

Asian / Male (A/M)

CHAPTER 4

WRITING CHRONOLOGICAL NARRATIVES

COMPETENCY 4: Construct a narrative report in a chronological format.

LEARNING OBJECTIVE 1: Distinguish between chronological and categorical formats.
LEARNING OBJECTIVE 2: Develop an introduction that identifies the author, nature, and time frame of the report.
LEARNING OBJECTIVE 3: Create a sequentially arranged body of the report.
LEARNING OBJECTIVE 4: Arrange subtopics and events by paragraph.
LEARNING OBJECTIVE 5: Articulate presence of criminal elements when applicable.
LEARNING OBJECTIVE 6: Identify venue in which the associated incident occurred.
LEARNING OBJECTIVE 7: Describe features of property, locations, and individuals through the use of physical characteristics.
LEARNING OBJECTIVE 8: Explain case disposition, investigative status, and follow-up necessities in a conclusion section.

Now that we've identified the characteristics of effective note-taking, it's time to consider how those notes will be incorporated into two basic types of police report narratives, chronological and categorical.

FACE SHEETS

Quality report writing requires time investment, something that police agencies have understood since the inception of the need to record information. To reduce the amount of time that reports take to write, many agencies have developed standardized report forms designed to capture nonnarrative, basic information about an event. These are called "face sheets." They are cover documents that give case information at a quick glance. These summary pages can include the report number, case type, location, date and time of incident, possible charges, and contact details for all involved parties.

Example: Sample Report Face Sheet

SAMPLE POLICE INCIDENT REPORT

Report Number: _____

Incident as Investigated:

Complainant:				Address:	
City:		State:		Home Phone:	
Sex:	Race:	DOB:		Work Phone:	

Reported By:				Address:	
City:		State:		Home Phone:	
Sex:	Race:	DOB:		Work Phone:	

Location of Incident:	Date and Time of Incident:	Date and Time Reported:

Vehicle involved: Yes ☐ No ☐	Complainant's ☐ Suspect's ☐	Year:	Make:	Model:	Type:	Style:
Color:	VIN / Hull Number:		License:	State:	Expires:	

Registered Owner:	Name:	Address:	City:	State:	Phone:

Vehicle Towed: Yes ☐ No ☐	If Yes, by who:	Location Taken:	At Whose Request:	Eligible for Release: Yes ☐ No ☐

Describe Injuries or Illness:	Hospital Used:	Transported By:	Admitted to Hospital: Yes ☐ No ☐

Suspect ☐ Witness ☐	Number:	Last Name:	First Name:	Middle:	Address:	City:	State:
Sex:	Race:	DOB:	Height:	Weight:	Hair:	Eyes:	Clothing Description:	Phone:

Arrested Yes ☐ No ☐	Charge:	Section Number:	Citation Number:

Suspect ☐ Witness ☐	Number:	Last Name:	First Name:	Middle:	Address:	City:	State:
Sex:	Race:	DOB:	Height:	Weight:	Hair:	Eyes:	Clothing Description:	Phone:

Arrested: Yes ☐ No ☐	Charge:	Section Number:	Citation Number:

Narrative: ☐ *see attached typed narrative*

Reporting Officer:	Assisting Officer(s):	Date of Report:	Approved By:

Cleared   Active   Inactive   Unfounded

Copies to: _____

Each agency will have its own summary cover sheets, and as such, officers should follow departmental policies when completing these important documents. Because of the lack of consistency in developed standardized report forms from agency to agency, this book focuses on the development of concise and informative report narratives, rather than to attempt to adapt lessons to the myriad report forms in existence.

TYPES OF REPORT NARRATIVES

There are two basic types of report narratives: chronological and categorical/topical.

Chronological narratives are sequential in nature. They are designed to follow a timeline of events that begins when an officer becomes aware of a possible situation and ends when the situation is either resolved or has been referred for further investigation.

Categorical narratives are designed to sort and isolate information based on the type or characteristics of that information. Report categories could include but are not limited to types of witnesses, types of evidence collected, types of crimes investigated, or locations of investigations. Categorical narratives will be addressed in further detail in Chapter 5.

> **Chronological Narrative**
> a sequential narrative used to describe a series of events, including what happened in an incident and the resulting actions taken by the police.

> **Categorical Narrative**
> a narrative based on the type of information being presented. It is used to highlight common characteristics of the persons, places, items, or actions described, forming groups of information.

CHRONOLOGICAL NARRATIVES

The most common type of report narrative you will write is the chronological narrative. These types of narratives can be used to accurately, briefly, and clearly address a wide range of police calls, from field interviews, to neighbor disputes, to traffic stops, to felonious matters such as a burglary or a homicide. Chronological reports will also be used in a variety of noncriminal or administrative matters noted in Chapter 2, such as memorandum/"In the matter of" reports, traffic crash reports, and use of force reports.

Chronological narratives, as the name implies, will articulate the series of events associated with an incident in the order that they occurred. These narratives will follow a structure similar to a format that you may be familiar with from writing essays in school: the opening, the body, and the conclusion. Each narrative should contain an opening, also known as an introduction. The next section comprises the body of the report subdivided by paragraphs that distinguish various facets of incident documentation (e.g., a different paragraph for each witness interviewed, each area searched, or each article of evidence processed). The final section of the report, or at least the final paragraph, should be the conclusion. This section should be used to explain resolution, or articulate any needed follow-up.

Opening/Introduction

Police professionals should become accustomed to including standardized basic information in the opening of any report. Such information should minimally include the day, date, and approximate time that an officer became aware of a situation. This should be followed by the identification of the officer (to include rank) and the officer's associated agency and assignment. It is also recommended that the officer identify whether the assignment involved being uniformed or nonuniformed.

Next, the means by which the officer became aware should be documented. There are three distinct ways in which an officer becomes aware of a situation: (1) the officer is dispatched, (2) the officer makes a direct observation, or (3) the officer is informed by a third party. This should be followed by the location of the incident or the reporting party, the nature of the incident (neighbor dispute, found property, theft complaint, traffic accident, etc.), and the **venue** in which the incident has occurred. Venue refers to the particular jurisdiction within which a certain event is located. In the following example, all of the previously discussed elements have been combined to form a thorough opening, or introductory, paragraph.

> *On Monday, November 3, 2012, at approximately 9:37 pm, I, Officer Kyle Smith, of the Watertown Police Department, assigned to Sqd. 18, in full uniform, was dispatched to the 1800 block of N. 14th St., in the City of Watertown, Dodge County, WI, for an "illegal fireworks" complaint.*

There are advantages and disadvantages that accompany the inclusion of venue in the introduction. The advantage is that the requirement to document venue is immediately addressed. The officer is then free to compose the remainder of the report without the risk of failing to articulate jurisdiction. On the other hand, there may be times when the area that the officer is initially directed to is in a jurisdiction different from that of the actual occurrence of the incident. In such cases, venue associated with the location of occurrence should be documented in the body of the report once that location has been identified.

Body

Writing Basics

The body of the report contains the main text of the report. Even though your report will be a legal, technical document, you need to make sure you are following generally accepted rules of good writing. For instance, be sure to write in simple sentences, making sure to avoid **run-on sentences.** Use words that your reader will understand. Avoid **jargon,** large words, and words that are difficult to pronounce. Always write in the **active voice,** and avoid using the passive voice. In a sentence using active voice, the subject of the sentence performs the action expressed in the verb (Toadvine et al., 2017). For example, "I assisted Smith as he changed his tire," sounds better than "Smith was assisted in the changing of his tire by me."

Venue

the particular jurisdiction within which a certain event is located.

Run-on sentences

a sentence containing two or more clauses not connected by the correct conjunction or punctuation (Merriam-Webster, 2017).

Jargon

using technical terms specific to policing that those outside of policing may not understand (Merriam-Webster, 2017).

Active voice

in a sentence using active voice, the subject of the sentence performs the action expressed in the verb

---

A GUIDE TO WRITING QUALITY POLICE REPORTS

Use consistent terminology. For example, if you are referring to the victim of a crime named Derrick Smith as "Smith" in your report, do not start referring to him as "Derrick," or "victim." On that same note, break up proper nouns with appropriately placed pronouns to make the report easier to read. For example, "Smith stated that he entered the building through the front door. He then immediately observed the suspect behind the counter, who then pointed a pistol at Smith," sounds better than, "Smith stated that Smith entered the building through the front door. Smith then immediately observed the suspect behind the counter, who then pointed a pistol at Smith."

Also, be sure to keep your report as short and simple as possible while maintaining the level of detail needed to accurately depict what happened. Avoid using excessive amounts of words, especially those that are used simply to make the report sound more official. For example, avoid writing things like "The alleged suspect vehicle in question was a Ford Mustang, 2017 model year, black in color." Instead, keep it simple: "The suspect vehicle was a black 2017 Ford Mustang."

Initial Considerations

In situations when approach considerations are an influential factor in officer response and/or may weigh heavily in the outcome of the incident, an initial paragraph of the body of the report should be composed to document those **approach considerations.** Additionally, the report should be a reflection of the officer's prioritization in response to an incident. In this way, a report can serve to reinforce that the officer prioritized properly in his or her response. Reports can be instrumental in after-action reviews, either formal (by the department) or informal (by the officer), to improve future responses.

> **Approach considerations**
> an officer's mental process of assessing variables associated with officer safety, conflict resolution and problem solving.

Just as the introduction establishes a base of information for the reader, so should the first sentence of the body. The officer should lead with arrival time and initial actions or observations. Quite often, agencies will have a standardized report form, or face sheet, that documents basic personal identifying information of people contacted throughout an investigation. The officer should develop a consistent method of collecting and documenting such information. In the event that an agency does not establish the identity of contacts by using a standardized form, the officer should provide initial, full, basic identifying information for each person referred to in the report. For the purposes of consistency, each time that such information is provided, it should be in the following order: last name, first name, middle initial, race, sex, date of birth, address, and phone number (see example).

Harrison, David, H.
White / Male, DOB 05-17-80
3247 S. Acre Way
Juneau, WI 53030
Phone: 920-386-4080

Once basic personal identifying information has been established, the identified person may thereafter be referred to by his or her last name. In the event that the incident involves multiple people who share the same last name, the officer should consider using both the first and last names of each individual, or, minimally, the first initial and last name. In cases where everyone related to an incident shares the same last name (such as in numerous domestic violence incidents), first names, without the use of the last name, may be used repeatedly once basic personal identifying information has been established.

In addition to basic personal identifying information, officers should identify any assisting or other responding units. This could include assisting officers, fire personnel, emergency medical services, or regulatory agencies. When describing these units, be sure to notate the squad/unit number, the agency of the squad/unit, the last names of the personnel on the unit, as well as the time the unit arrived on scene.

When transporting anyone from the scene of an incident, information identifying who the transporting unit is, as well as the time of transport, destination, and who the transported party was turned over to should be documented.

This may sound as if an overabundance of information is being gathered, but keep in mind, police reports are designed to paint a picture of what happened in the mind of the person who was not there to make observations for themselves. Often, such reports are not referred to for months or even years after the information has been collected. Therefore, it is critical that reports are as thorough, within reason, as possible when they are initially composed. Also, it may be necessary to recontact responding personnel at some future date, to gather further information or to utilize them as witnesses. Therefore, documenting their identification, at the time of the event, is critical.

Sequence of Investigation

In addition to documenting who was interviewed and what other units responded, you also have to lay out the sequence of your investigation. Think of it as telling a story. Hundreds of times a day, people relay stories about their experiences. Those attentive to such stories understand them because they generally follow a logical sequence from the beginning, to the circumstances as they unfolded, followed by the ending, or closure. With an understanding of human nature in relation to storytelling and receiving, it is important that we apply those most fundamental principles in formulating police reports.

In a chronological narrative, the story you will be telling in your report is simply the story of what happened during an incident. You will develop this story through the process of interviewing the victims, witnesses, suspects, and complainants to gather information about the incident from the perspective of all parties involved. Please understand that some of these stories may not always be the same; everyone views an incident from their own perspective and, because of this, may perceive the situation to be slightly different from the account expressed by others who viewed the exact same incident. It is your job to document a factual account of the incident, committing the statements of the victims, witnesses, suspects, and complainants to record.

Additionally, you will be reviewing and documenting any video evidence that may be available of an incident. This evidence may serve to corroborate or contradict the statements of victims, witnesses, suspects, and complainants. You will also be documenting any physical evidence on scene. This may include evidence you are able to collect and keep, such as shell casings, bodily fluids, or money, and evidence you are unable to collect and keep, such as tire skid marks, damage to property, paint transfer, and tool marks. While you may not be able to collect these types of evidence, you can photograph and/or make video of them. In this case, you will need to note the presence of the photographs/video, as well as compose a photograph log which will document the contents of each photograph.

As this is a chronological narrative, used to tell a story, start from the beginning, describing the circumstances leading up to your arrival on scene as noted above. Document your interviews in the order completed. Articulate the contents of each interview, even if it is reporting the same information that was articulated in an interview with another witness. The best stories contain a rich level of detail. The same is true of the best police reports. Be sure to collect a high level of detail when conducting interviews, and be sure to document that in your notes. Never assume the answer to a question. Do not be reluctant to ask what you might consider to be a "stupid" question; it is not your job to look smart, it is your job to gather as much detail about an incident as possible. Document all of this detail into your report to illustrate the incident's story as fully as possible.

Elements of the Crime

When writing a crime-related narrative, officers need to be aware of the elements of the crime in question and be sure to articulate those elements into their report. The elements of a crime are the characteristics of an act which must be present to prove that a crime occurred. These need to be covered in the body of your report. By doing so, you will ensure that the facts of the investigation either substantiate the elements of a specific crime or explain that the circumstances investigated do not rise to the level of criminal activity.

Consider the elements of burglary in Wisconsin:

> WI §§. 943.10 (1) (a) Burglary: Intentionally entering a building or dwelling, without the consent of the person in lawful possession and with the intent to steal or commit a felony.

In the case of an officer investigating a suspected burglary, the officer would need to articulate the following elements into the report:

1. Entering a building or dwelling
2. Doing so intentionally
3. Doing so without consent of the possessor (i.e., owner)
4. Doing so with the intent to steal or commit a felony

If an officer is able to articulate all four of these points (elements), then he or she would be able to refer the case for prosecution after identifying a suspect. Failure to articulate any of the four elements would preclude prosecution for burglary and justify the officer or department in not taking action or arresting a suspect for that crime.

Description of Property

When describing lost, found, stolen, damaged, or missing property, include a description of the item(s), specifically the quantity of items, the type and style of each item, physical description, color, condition, and value. The officer should also identify any trade names, logos, or identifying numbers, marks, or initials engraved in, or affixed to, an item.

Boilerplate Language

Boilerplate language
standardized or set language that is meant to be used repeatedly, often in organizational publications or legal documents.

Boilerplate language is defined as standardized or set language that is meant to be used repeatedly, often in organizational publications or legal documents (*American Heritage Dictionary, 2017*). Such language is both acceptable and desirable in its application to legal documents, such as search warrant applications, because the basic categorical elements of various types of search warrants (types and characteristics of evidence to be seized) change very little from case to case. The specific details of a search warrant application, such as suspect names, address locations, vehicle descriptions, and actions taken should be documented in a report narrative independent of boilerplate language. However, when documenting an event, an investigation, or a situational response, officers should avoid the use of boilerplate language for a number of reasons. Generally, although many situations may be similar, no two are exactly the same. Therefore, inappropriate use of boilerplate language fails to capture the unique characteristics of individual situations; may create gaps in factual reporting; precludes vital, factual information from later consideration; and could diminish the credibility of the officer.

Concluding Paragraph

The concluding paragraph is used to explain the resolution of an incident. This is an opportunity for the reporting officer to articulate unresolved issues, convey the status of an investigation, or document referral to services or specialized investigative bodies. No new information is presented in the conclusion (Wells & Brizee, 2017). Instead, the reporting officer sums up what has been written so far, articulates any needed follow-up, and/or puts into words the disposition of the case. Any disposition will have to include the disposition of individuals arrested, as well as the disposition of any evidence collected. The goal of the conclusion is to wrap up the report in a logical manner, leaving the reader with a complete picture of (a) what happened in the case; (b) what happened to victims, witnesses, suspects, complainants, and property; and (c) what is left to be done to complete the investigation (Wells & Brizee, 2017)).

CONCLUSION

The vast majority of reports that you will write will contain a chronological narrative. The ability to describe what happened in an incident, in the order that events occurred, is crucial to many types of reports. Following the basic format of introduction–body–conclusion helps to structure the report in a way that is easier to write. It is also a format that most people have been taught throughout all levels of education, making it easier for readers to follow. The next chapter will describe categorical narratives, another type of narrative designed to help make reports easier to understand.

ACTIVITY: CITIZEN CONTACT (FIELD INTERVIEW)

Student Instructions:

For this activity, please partner with a classmate. You will play the role of an officer on patrol. Your classmate will play the role of an individual who is walking around a used car lot at 12:30 am. The individual is peering into various cars and trying the door handles in an apparent attempt to enter several of them. A number of times, the individual appears to duck down between the vehicles and then reappear moments later.

Remember to use your professional communication skills while gathering information and all throughout the contact. In addition, during the information-gathering process, take concise field notes. Use those field notes to complete the Citizen Contact form that is attached to this activity. Complete the Citizen Contact (Field Interview) form below based on the information gathered during contact with the suspicious person. Along with the blank Citizen Contact form, a completed example has been provided for you. If necessary, be prepared to show your work and ask clarifying questions in class.

This contact will be classified as a "Field Interview."

The address of the used car lot is 9175 W. Lexington Drive, Appleton, WI 54911.

Incident Report #: 18-8264327

Officer ID#: 3321

Classmate role: _You work second shift and get off at midnight. Recently, your family's only car broke down, so you have been investigating the possibility of purchasing a new one. Before work every day, you are responsible for caring for your two children while your wife is at work. You are cooperative with the officer who approaches you._

CITIZEN CONTACT REPORT

INCIDENT NO.

OFFENSE REPORT	Y ☐	N ☐
JUVENILE	Y ☐	N ☐
SCHOOL		GRADE

| NAME - LAST | FIRST | MIDDLE | AKA/NICKNAME |
| ADDRESS | | CITY, STATE, ZIP | PHONE |

| BIRTHDATE | M ☐ F ☐ | WHI. ☐ BLK. ☐ NAT.AM. ☐ ASN. ☐ HISP. ☐ | HEIGHT | WEIGHT | HAIR | EYES |

SCARS, MARKS, TATTOOS LOCATIONS/DESCRIPTION — PARENTS

DRIVER'S LICENSE	STATE	EXP.	SOCIAL SECURITY #	PROB./PAR. Y ☐ N ☐
VEH. PLATE/VIN	EXP.	STATE	MAKE	YEAR	MODEL	COLOR
DATE OF OFFENSE	TIME	LOCATION OF OFFENSE

CONTACT NARRATIVE

| SIGNATURE OF CONTACTED PERSON | OFFICER SIGNATURE | OFFICER NO. |

GANG INFO - GANG NAME — STATUS: MEMBER ☐ ASSOCIATE ☐ SUSPECTED ☐ — GANG MEMBER ID CRITERIA 1 2 3 4 5 6 7 CIRCLE APPLICABLE NUMBERS

ASSOCIATES — BIRTHDATE — ADDRESS — PHONE
1)
2)

TYPE OF CONTACT
- ☐ 1 WARNING: City Ordinance Violation. Failure to correct or comply can result in legal action being commenced against you.
- ☐ 2 WARNING: Vehicle Traffic Law Violation. You have violated a traffic law that is described in the narrative section of this notice.
- ☐ 3 VEHICLE DEFECT: The violation(s) indicated must be corrected at once. ALL FUTURE OPERATIONS WITHOUT CORRECTION ARE ILLEGAL.
- ☐ 4 BICYCLE VIOLATION
- ☐ 5 FIELD INTERROGATION
- ☐ 6 REPORT IN PERSON: Report to the Police Department
- ☐ 7 OTHER CONTACT
- ☐ Within 15 days sign this notice and mail or bring it to the _____ Police Department, unless you are instructed to report in person. FAILURE TO COMPLY CAN RESULT IN ARREST ACTION AGAINST YOU.

I CERTIFY THAT THE LISTED VIOLATION(S) HAVE BEEN CORRECTED:

SIGNATURE — CERTIFICATION — DATE

DEPARTMENT COPY

CITIZEN CONTACT REPORT

INCIDENT NO. 00-000-00

OFFENSE REPORT	Y ☐	N ☒
JUVENILE	Y ☐	N ☒
SCHOOL		GRADE

NAME - LAST	FIRST	MIDDLE	AKA/NICKNAME
Rupiper	Brian	X.	"Pipe"
ADDRESS		CITY, STATE, ZIP	PHONE
7453 Union Grove Dr.		Mayville WI 57163	920-984-5553

| BIRTHDATE | M ☒ F ☐ | WHI. ☒ BLK. ☐ NAT.AM. ☐ ASN. ☐ HISP. ☐ | HEIGHT | WEIGHT | HAIR | EYES |
| 08-04-80 | | | 6'1" | 180 | BRO | BLU |

SCARS, MARKS, TATTOOS LOCATIONS/DESCRIPTION: Tattoo of "Pipe" L. Upper Arm — PARENTS: Deceased

DRIVER'S LICENSE	STATE	EXP.	SOCIAL SECURITY #	PROB./PAR. Y ☐ N ☒
R000-6152-0404-02	WI	09	393-72-3142	
VEH. PLATE/VIN	EXP.	STATE	MAKE	YEAR	MODEL	COLOR
PYP MAN	03	WI	Ford	1999	2 dr	SIL
DATE OF OFFENSE	TIME	LOCATION OF OFFENSE
08-18-02	0300	417 Commercial Way

CONTACT NARRATIVE

I saw Rupiper looking in a jewelry store window with a flashlight. He ducked into the shadows as I approached.

| SIGNATURE OF CONTACTED PERSON | OFFICER SIGNATURE | OFFICER NO. |
| Brian Rupiper | P.O. Joe Williams | 5617 |

GANG INFO - GANG NAME — STATUS: MEMBER ☐ ASSOCIATE ☐ SUSPECTED ☐ — GANG MEMBER ID CRITERIA 1 2 3 4 5 6 7 8 CIRCLE APPLICABLE NUMBERS

ASSOCIATES — BIRTHDATE — ADDRESS — PHONE
1)
2)

TYPE OF CONTACT
- ☐ 1 WARNING: City Ordinance Violation. Failure to correct or comply can result in legal action being commenced against you.
- ☐ 2 WARNING: Vehicle Traffic Law Violation. You have violated a traffic law that is described in the narrative section of this notice.
- ☐ 3 VEHICLE DEFECT: The violation(s) indicated must be corrected at once. ALL FUTURE OPERATIONS WITHOUT CORRECTION ARE ILLEGAL.
- ☐ 4 BICYCLE VIOLATION
- ☒ 5 FIELD INTERROGATION
- ☐ 6 REPORT IN PERSON: Report to the Police Department
- ☐ 7 OTHER CONTACT
- ☐ Within 15 days sign this notice and mail or bring it to the _____ Police Department, unless you are instructed to report in person. FAILURE TO COMPLY CAN RESULT IN ARREST ACTION AGAINST YOU.

I CERTIFY THAT THE LISTED VIOLATION(S) HAVE BEEN CORRECTED:

SIGNATURE — CERTIFICATION — DATE

DEPARTMENT COPY

A GUIDE TO WRITING QUALITY POLICE REPORTS

ACTIVITY: REPORT NARRATIVE INTRODUCTION PARAGRAPH

For each set of circumstances provided, place them in the proper order, in the format of a brief paragraph, on the lines provided. Information should be written as it would appear in the introduction paragraph of a narrative police report. Use the examples below as a guide.

<u>Dispatched Call</u>

Example:
*On Saturday, November 3, 2018, at approximately 9:37 pm, I, Officer Kyle Smith, assigned to Sqd. 18, in full uniform, **was dispatched** to the 1800 block of N. 14th St. for an "illegal fireworks" complaint.*

_____ Saturday, February 10, 2018

_____ Loud Noise Complaint

_____ full uniform

_____ Sqd. 23

_____ 77 Elkwood Terrace

_____ Dispatched: 4:53 pm

_____ Theft of speakers

_____ Sqd. 98

_____ Dispatched: 10:20 am

_____ Wednesday, May 9, 2018

_____ 1452 Robin Way

_____ full uniform

_____ Sqd. 36

_____ Friday, April 27, 2018

_____ Suspicious person

_____ 894 E. 8th St. (Complainant)

_____ full uniform

_____ Dispatched: 9:08 pm

_____ full uniform

_____ Dispatched: 6:37 am

_____ Tuesday, June 12, 2018

_____ Gas Drive-off

_____ MotoMart, 6309 E. 4th St.

_____ Sqd. 819

Incident Reported by Citizen Approach

Example:

On Tuesday, December 11, 2018, at approximately 4:47 pm, I, Officer Jason Bentley, assigned to Sqd. 53B, in full uniform, **_was approached_** _by John C. Erickson, w/m, 04-14-47, of 832 W. Haven Ct., Ph. (920) 832-4740, who reported that kids were fighting in the 1300 block of N. Ocean Drive._

Use names listed below as complainants in the following report activity iterations.

Subject Names and Info:

Elliott, Donald P. Black / Male DOB: 07-29-1987 4567 Warnimont Pl. Bixford, WI, 54327 Ph: (920) 228-1368	Wesson, Vicky L Hispanic / Female DOB: 02-27-1973 8935 Market Square Tipton, WI 53888 (715) 821-7908	Calderone, Vincent X. Hispanic / Male DOB: 01-03-1969 7 Spartan Ct. Wilbur, WI 59712 (920) 671-7745
Thao, Tong (nmi) Asian / Male DOB: 05-11-1986 1210 Victor Lane Clement, WI 53442 Ph: (715) 491-6148		**nmi** an abbreviation for "no middle initial." This is used when a subject does not have a middle name.

_____ 8:45 pm

_____ Citizen report of accident

_____ Intersection, 3rd and Main

_____ full uniform

_____ Sqd. 76R

_____ Saturday, July 14, 2018

_____ Citizen report of

_____ Kids painting graffiti on wall

_____ Sunday, August 5, 2018

_____ full uniform

_____ Union Church, 505 N. 8th St.

_____ 6:32 pm

_____ Sqd. 28C

_____ 8700 block N. Homestead Dr.

_____ Sqd. 11

_____ 11:17 pm

_____ Citizen report of gang fight

_____ Thursday, October 4, 2018

_____ full uniform

_____ 5400 block of Congress St.

_____ Monday, January 29, 2018

_____ full uniform

_____ 12:13 pm

_____ Sqd. 68D

_____ Citizen report of incapacitated person

<u>Incident Observed by Officer</u>

Example

On Thursday, May 17, 2017, at approximately 4:15 am, I, Officer Richard Tess, while assigned to Sqd. 732D and on patrol in full uniform, **<u>observed</u>** a fight between two men in front of 4312 S. 13th St. I immediately notified dispatch and called for back-up.

_____ Sqd. 83B

_____ Sunday, September 2, 2018

_____ Alley-3400 block Elm St.

_____ Sound of breaking glass

_____ 3:40 am

_____ full uniform

_____ Loud argument

_____ 9:30 pm

_____ Saturday, November 24, 2018

_____ Sqd. 49

_____ full uniform

_____ Park and ride lot, Hwy 13 and Mill Rd.

_____ full uniform

_____ Sqd. 114S

_____ 4700 block W. Holly Rd.

_____ 3:50 am

_____ Man carrying television

_____ Monday, April 9, 2018

_____ Wednesday, Feb. 28, 2018

_____ 100 block Armistead Dr.

_____ Sqd. 63B

_____ One-car collision

_____ full uniform

_____ 2:43 am

ACTIVITY: BODY OF THE REPORT NARRATIVE

In preparation for writing the body of a report, for each set of circumstances provided below, determine the chronological sequence of events by numbering each line in order of occurrence. Then construct a short narrative that includes all elements of the event in chronological order. Each new topic (suspect interview, witness interview, evidence collection, etc.) should be presented in its own paragraph.

You have been dispatched to the report of a "Fight on the Playground," Jackson Pollock Middle School 4281 W. Fulton Ave. Use the information below to construct the body of the report.

_____ You administer a cold compress to Thomson's left eye

_____ Victor F. Adams, white / male, 03-08-2000, 5516 N. Oak St., Verona, WI 52771, Ph. (608) 873-4501 said that Thomson called his mother a slimy swamp beast. Thomson then threw a rock at him (Adams). Thomson then ran up to Adams and punched him in the stomach. Adams said he punched Thomson back, once in the stomach and once in the face, before the police showed up.

_____ You call for backup and separate the two boys.

_____ You arrive at 6:37 pm and see two young boys rolling on the ground with each other while exchanging punches.

_____ You give Adams a gauze pad to use to help stop his bloody nose.

_____ Eric R. Thompson, White / Male, 07-13-2007, 3314 Weston Ct., Verona, WI 52771, Ph. (715) 553-8826 said that he and Adams were arguing about who was a better kickball player when Adams told Thomson that he plays like an old lady. Thomson told Adams to leave him alone. That's when Adams punched Thomson in the left eye.

_____ You ask Thomson if he ever said anything to Adams about his mother. Thomson said that he might have said something about her living in a swamp.

_____ Back-up Sqd, 63 (Carver) arrived at 6:39 pm and stayed with Adams while you interview Thomson about what had happened.

_____

_____

_____

_____

_____

_____

In preparation for writing the body of a report, for each set of circumstances provided below, determine the chronological sequence of events by numbering each line in order of occurrence. Then construct a short narrative that includes all elements of the event in chronological order. Each new topic (suspect interview, witness interview, evidence collection, etc.) should be presented in its own paragraph.

You have been dispatched to the report of an "Injured Person" lying on the sidewalk at 1417 S. Monroe St. Use the information below to construct the body of the report.

_____ The witness, William M. Robinson, w/m, 3-17-77, 2418 Martin Dr., Barlow, WI 53336, Ph. (920) 818-1973, saw a man on a flatbed truck tossing bags off the truck bed to a man on the sidewalk. The man on the sidewalk was stacking bags on a cart. A lady walked between the two men. The man on the truck, without looking first, tossed a bag toward the man on the sidewalk. A lady was walking north and got hit in the head with the bag that was tossed.

_____ At 3:17 pm you call for EMS and dispatch informs you that Gold Cross Ambulance is already en route.

_____ At 3:35 pm you checked the area for any additional witnesses to the incident but found none.

_____ You retrieve your first-aid kit, check to see if the victim, Elaine V. Samuels, b/f, 04-26-79, 3819 Wendell Ave., Barlow, WI 53334, Ph. (920)453-6625, who is lying on the ground, is conscious and breathing. You discover that she is. You ask her what happened. She says that she got hit in the head by a sandbag. She says that her head hurts. You ask her if she knows what the date and approximate time is and she accurately tells you. You check for any other injuries, and ask triage information (allergies, medical conditions).

_____ Carl H. Wilson, b/m, 01-29-85, 865 E. 8th St., Barlow, WI 53336, Ph. (920)221-9450 was on the truck. He tossed a bag of concrete off the truck to Jensen. Wilson heard a scream and someone yelled, "Oh my god, get some help!"

_____ Arrived 3:16 pm, met the caller, Sandra K. Iverson, h/f, 10-02-73, 1900 Monroe St., Barlow, WI 53336, Ph. (920)712-3484. Caller was walking south on Munroe in front of 1417. 1417 is the address of the County Concrete Company's warehouse. Caller saw two men unloading bags of concrete mix from a flatbed truck. One of the men tossed a bag off the truck toward the other man. The bag hit a lady who was walking next to the truck, knocking her to the ground. The lady didn't get up. One of the men from the truck yelled for someone to call 911.

_____ You ask a person in the gathering crowd, Randy J. Caffrey, w/m, 2-13-75, 295 Allen Circle, Barlow, WI 53336, Ph. (920)221-4863 to monitor the victim until EMS arrives and he agrees. You tell him to inform you if her status (conscious and breathing) changes.

_____ At 3:23 pm Gold Cross Ambulance (Williams and Delaney) arrived to medically care for the victim.

_____ Todd C. Jenson, w/m, 04-14-82, 6310 Arlington Way, Barlow, WI 53334, Ph. (920)546-0087 saw the woman coming, tried to warn Wilson, but he had already tossed the bag.

A GUIDE TO WRITING QUALITY POLICE REPORTS

ACTIVITY: NARRATIVE CONCLUSION/ DISPOSITION PARAGRAPH

Instructions: For each line below indicate which section of a report narrative they belong in by placing "I" (introduction), "B" (body), or "C" (conclusion) in the associated blanks. Then, using only the lines classified as "C," construct a concluding paragraph. Use the example below as a guide.

Example:

__B__ Interviewed David Wilson, 4167 Jonathan Drive who neither heard nor saw anyone suspicious.

__C__ Case has been referred to Detective Unit 114 for follow-up investigation.

__B__ I discovered broken glass fragments and a brick lying on the floor in the center of the southeast bedroom.

__C__ I downloaded 18 pictures of the scene from the Squad 18 camera to the department "Pictures" drive.

__B__ I collected a plaster cast of the footprint, packaged it and inventoried it at the police department (see inventory 883261).

__I__ Dispatched at 4:57 pm to 4165 Jonathan Drive for the sound of breaking glass.

__B__ Discovered a footprint in the soft dirt outside the window of the southeast bedroom.

__C__ Made a roll-call board entry for squads to increase patrol in the area.

__B__ Knocked at the door of 4163 Jonathan Drive in an attempt to interview the neighbor of the victim, but received no answer.

__B__ Photographs of the scene, including footprint and the brick, were taken by Squad 18.

__C__ All evidence collected was inventoried and secured in the department evidence room.

Upon completion of my initial investigation, I downloaded 18 pictures of the scene from the Squad 18 camera to the department "Pictures" drive. I then made a roll-call board entry for squads to increase patrol in the area. All evidence collected was inventoried and secured in the department evidence room. This case has been referred to Detective Unit 114 for follow-up investigation.

_____ Jason Bentley was released to his mother Joan at 1:54 am.

_____ I was met at the door by the resident, Ricky W. Franklin, who allowed me in.

_____ I inventoried the half-barrel of beer as evidence (see Inventory # 94652).

_____ Contacted Joan C. Bentley and asked her to pick up her son Jason.

_____ At 12:23 am responded to the report of an underage drinking party at 8342 North Shore Ct.

_____ Issued Citation #586312 to Bentley for underage possession of alcohol.

_____ I interviewed Jason Bentley, 02-26-97 who admitted to drinking three cups of beer.

_____ I explained the reason for the citation, the deposit amount, and the court date to Joan Bentley.

_____ Sqd. 37 (VanDyke) was positioned at the back of the residence as I made contact at the front door.

_____ I observed a half-barrel of Miller Genuine Draft sitting in a large red bucket of ice in the kitchen.

_____

_____

_____

_____

_____

_____

_____

_____

_____

_____

_____

_____

_____

_____

_____

_____

_____

_____

_____ McAllister was confined on the charge of Operating a Motor Vehicle While Intoxicated

_____ The vehicle was searched by backup squad 93 (Cranston) and one Seagram's wine cooler bottle was discovered under the driver's seat.

_____ I observed a red, Buick, Regal, southbound on 17th St. from Addison Drive.

_____ I placed her in handcuffs and searched her.

_____ McAllister failed the Walk and Turn Test.

_____ The vehicle was towed by Bulldog Towing to their holding facility.

_____ The vehicle swerved across the centerline three times within one block and failed to stop for the stop sign at Main St.

_____ She failed to follow instructions and turned her head several times during the HGN test.

_____ I inventoried the Seagram's wine cooler bottle at the police station (see Inventory # 00231452).

_____ The vehicle hit the curb when I signaled it to pull over.

_____ Upon failing the Standardized Field Sobriety Tests, I told McAllister that she was under arrest for Operating a Motor Vehicle While Intoxicated.

_____ I smelled the strong odor of an alcoholic beverage on her breath.

_____ McAllister was unable to perform the One-Leg-Stand test.

_____ At 3:23 am I transported McAllister to the Calumet County Jail where I turned her over to Deputy Billings.

_____

_____

_____

_____

_____

_____

_____

_____

_____

_____

CHAPTER 5

CATEGORICAL NARRATIVES

COMPETENCY 5: Construct a narrative report in a categorical format.

LEARNING OBJECTIVE 1: Distinguish between chronological and categorical formats.
LEARNING OBJECTIVE 2: Identify categories/subcategories to be described within the Report.
LEARNING OBJECTIVE 3: Arrange categories/subcategories by paragraph.
LEARNING OBJECTIVE 4: Describe features of property, locations, and individuals through the use of physical characteristics.
LEARNING OBJECTIVE 5: Explain case disposition, investigative status, and follow-up when applicable.

As noted in the previous chapter, the vast majority of police reports will have chronological narratives. This is because they are a reflection of how we naturally process stories and events. Categorical narratives are different from chronological narratives in that they do not reflect a chronology of events. Rather, they isolate various segments of the larger story by category, that is, by class, group, or type. Unless there is a specific call for a categorical narrative, the officer should default to a chronological narrative format. Because of this, categorical narratives are used infrequently. However, when faced with a situation that requires this type of report, it is important that you understand what it is, as well as how to best use one.

Perhaps the most common application of a categorical narrative would be as a supplement to a larger investigative document utilized to record a specific element of the investigation. Consider the following situation: A drug investigation uncovers a network of three locations through which a single drug lord is carrying out operations. Multiple search warrants are obtained and as the primary investigator is searching one of the locations of the network, she sends separate officers to the other two locations. Each of those officers could submit a categorical narrative documenting the evidence found at their respective locations that would serve as supplements to the primary investigator's report. Such a supplement might look, in part, like the following example.

<u>Living room</u>

- (12) plastic sandwich bags with 1 corner of each bag removed
- (1) OHaus scale with white powdery residue on the table of the scale

<u>Bedroom</u>

- (1) .22 caliber revolver
- $700.00 in cash

<u>Kitchen</u>

- (1) ledger containing names, amounts of substances delivered, and prices paid for each

As with chronological narratives, it is important to bear in mind the basics of good writing. Write in simple sentences, consider your audience and use words they will understand, use lists articulated in a logical order (e.g., chronological or alphabetical), use consistent terminology, keep it short and simple, and use active voice. Also, be sure that your categories are logical. A categorical narrative is designed to make large amounts of information easier to digest by establishing categories as a frame of reference for the reader.

On the subject of logical categories, it is important to note that in categorical narratives, you will be using headings to separate categories. Note in the example above, there is the main heading of **Items discovered at 340 Hummingbird Drive**, followed by the subheadings of *Living Room*, *Bedroom*, and *Kitchen*. These heading serve to clearly express to the reader where the items noted were found.

CONCLUSION

Whether writing a categorical or chronological narrative, the importance of reviewing what you have written cannot be overstated. Often, writers (including this author) may believe that they have written a draft that represents factual thought without error, only to discover, upon review of what was written, that errors have inadvertently been made. In the chapter to follow, report revision will be discussed in detail.

CHAPTER 6

REVISING

> **COMPETENCY 6:** Improve the quality of a report through revision of a previous draft.

> **LEARNING OBJECTIVE 1:** Screen a report draft for accuracy, validity, and consistency.
> **LEARNING OBJECTIVE 2:** Recognize wordy content.
> **LEARNING OBJECTIVE 3:** Modify content to be concise.
> **LEARNING OBJECTIVE 4:** Develop report with regard for the associated users.

To this point, we have discussed the gathering of factual information and the type of report developed, relative to the purpose intended by the writer. Throughout this chapter, the various considerations in the review and revision of a report will be highlighted. Officers should direct particular attention to accuracy, validity-relevance, consistency, conciseness, and consideration of audience. Ultimately, revision involves adding or deleting material and adjusting sentences and paragraphs to make the narrative flow better.

ACCURACY

We live in the electronic age! Although the technological advancement of police practices varies from agency to agency, many departments now rely on the use of video and audio recordings to gather and preserve evidence. The savvy report writer will review the recorded document of an incident. Information documented in the recordings may be referenced in the written documentation and used to augment the officer's report. Reviewing video will also afford you the opportunity to recall details you may have unintentionally left out of your report (i.e., things you forgot to mention) due to the complex and dynamic nature of police encounters. You will note that sometimes there will be subtle differences between your recollection and what is captured on video. This is natural. Video recording is a two-dimensional visual medium trying to capture a multidimensional, multisensory world. Even though there may be an apparent discrepancy between the officer's recollection and what is observable in the video, the officer should not exclude his or her recollection from the report, but rather qualify it as "officer perception." Remember that the Supreme Court tells us in **Graham v. Connor** that officer perceptions, training, and experience are very important when determining the reasonableness of police action. Therefore, be sure to include your recollection and perceptions in your report as they will be invaluable to explaining the video.

VALIDITY

Relevance

Another point to consider is whether the information you have included in the report is valid, that is, relevant to the topic at hand. Sort out details that are pertinent to the incident from peripheral, irrelevant, or nonessential details (i.e., information that is not related directly to the report, that diverts the attention of the reader and dilutes the usefulness of the report).

Imagine reading a report in which the officer had documented her investigation of a traffic accident. As she gathered information, she interviewed people standing around the scene as possible witnesses. In addition to each interviewee's personal identification information, she also documented that one was eating a sandwich (possibly bologna), another smelled of cologne, one person was wearing a gold necklace and another was wearing strapless sandals. The accident was relatively minor (superficial paint transfer and small dents). The driver statements reflected slightly different accounts of what had led up to the accident making the interview of possible witnesses necessary to gather a more accurate account of what had happened. Considering the totality of circumstances, documenting information such as "eating a sandwich, smelling of cologne, wearing a gold necklace or strapless sandals," although factual, is irrelevant to the investigation. While collection and documentation of detailed information about an incident is an important part of report writing, it is equally important that officers leave out details that have nothing to do with the case.

Facts vs. Opinions

According to *Merriam-Webster Dictionary* (2017), a fact is a piece of information presented as having objective reality. Facts are things that could be observed by others, things that others could use to form an opinion. An opinion, on the other hand, is a view, judgment, or appraisal formed in the mind about a particular matter. Opinions may or may not be substantiated by fact.

Officers must avoid including unsubstantiated opinions in their reports. Unsubstantiated opinions are those made without reference to evidence. While it is completely acceptable for an officer to state an opinion, that opinion must be clearly linked to factual information. Consider the following statements:

- "I discovered marijuana."
- "He had alcohol on his breath."

Both of these are opinions; they lead the informed reader to question how the officer knew that the substance was marijuana, or how the officer could smell an odorless liquid on a subject's breath. These statements would be better articulated in terms of the facts the officer observed:

- "I discovered a green leafy substance in a small clear plastic baggie. Based on my training and experience, the substance smelled like raw marijuana."
- "When the subject spoke, I detected a strong odor of intoxicants on his breath."

Although these statements of fact may appear to violate the rule of being concise while writing (addressed next chapter), they are far more factually accurate than original statements of opinion, and therefore would be the correct information to be included in a police report.

Also, officers need to avoid editorializing, that is, including personal statements of opinion about a subject or an incident. For example, a statement such as, "The suspect made another brilliant decision and decided to run," is sarcastically judgmental about the subject's intelligence, and has nothing to do with the facts of the case. Officers must avoid letting their personal feelings inhibit the objectivity of their job performance, including their reports.

Officers are also cautioned to avoid including assumptions in their reports as well as in their investigations. Assumptions are like opinions—that is, they are not based on fact. For example, "No one answered the door, therefore no one was home" is an assumption, whereas "No one answered the door" is a fact. Officers must avoid assumptions just like they must avoid editorializing. When officers include their assumptions in reports, they are simply highlighting their mistakes and misses in the information-gathering process.

So far, we have described at length the need for officers to include factual information in their reports. There is an area, however, where officers have to be very careful in the factual information they relate: identifying information on confidential informants. Confidential informants are individuals who are providing information to the police on a confidential, or secret, basis to protect their identity. If the identities of confidential informants are discovered, it could potentially place their health, safety, and well-being in danger. When writing a report involving information obtained from a confidential informant, officers need to make sure they are following all relevant federal, state, and local laws, as well as agency policy.

A note on witness observations: Imagine that during the processing of a crime scene, photos are taken of a black, semiautomatic pistol lying 10 feet (as measured) away from a vehicle. The information in the photograph represents the objective reality of what was discovered at the scene and is therefore factual. Now, suppose that three witnesses to the placement of the gun were interviewed. Two witnesses claim that a front, right passenger of the vehicle in the photo ran from the car and, in doing so, dropped the gun on the ground. The third witness claims that the driver was the one who dropped the gun after getting out of the car via the driver's door and running around the back of the car. All three witness statements represent opinions based on their respective recollections of their observations, but the only information that could be claimed as factual in this situation is what has actually been depicted in the photograph. Therefore, officers should avoid assumption about what is, or is not, fact. A fact must be qualified in nature and be indisputable. Until that is established, officers must remember that witness observations are merely opinions.

CONSISTENCY

Your report must also be consistent with available information—that is, your information should be the same across the various documents, such as field notes, diagrams, photographs, and recordings associated with a case. As noted, there may be subtle differences between your recollections and what is captured on video. The same is true for audio recordings as well as photographic evidence. Your report is your chance to explain those discrepancies in writing.

During the initial composition of your report, you should have been reviewing your notes to help jog your memory and increase your accuracy. Your process of revision should also include a comparison between what you wrote and what you have in your notes. Consistency between your notes and your report is important. Depending on your jurisdiction, your notes may be discoverable in court. As with video and audio recordings, inconsistencies between your notes and your report can cast doubt on the accuracy of your report.

There will be times when you are called upon to make a drawing of a scene. This could be a drawing of a simple traffic crash scene, a street scene (documenting criminal damage caused over a two-block long area), or a drawing of a crime scene inside a building. In these cases, this drawing will be used to help those reading your report understand the incident by providing a visual aid. It is important that your drawing be consistent with what you are expressing in your report, and what you have documented in your notes. The old saying is, "A picture is worth a thousand words." Drawings that are inconsistent with what is listed in a report will just lead to confusion, thereby casting doubt on the accuracy of your report.

As noted in the previous section "Validity" (under "Fact vs. Opinion"), witness statements may be inconsistent. Remember that unlike you, most witnesses are not trained observers. They are not trained to be aware of what is occurring in their environment. They are usually not inclined to carry a notebook with them or to write down notes about what they saw in a given incident. So while witness observations are not necessarily factual, they are representative of witness perceptions based on the recollection of their observations, and therefore must be noted in your report. This is true even if they are inconsistent on some points. The job of the police is to document, and then sift out fact from opinion, in an attempt to determine what happened in an incident. As with the other points on consistency, your report is an opportunity to explain minor inconsistencies between and among your witness statements. For instance, if two witnesses give a different color for the same car, and one of the witnesses is color blind, their perceptions of the car color may be different. In this case, it would be important to document the witness's colorblindness as it is relevant to the witness's observation, and will serve to help explain inconsistency in witness statements.

CONCISENESS

Being concise means that you are making every word count. Reports that are concise express all needed information, without using more words than are necessary. Consider these two examples:

Nonconcise: After securing the burglary scene, I canvassed the area for possible witnesses to the incident. As a result, I interviewed three witnesses. The first witness, Kent Jones, at 1417 Maple Street, said that he slept through the night and did not see or hear anything other than the late show that was on T.V. at the approximate time that he had fallen asleep. Another possible witness at 1423 Maple Street, Ashley Williams said that she was out of town the day that the burglary occurred, but had heard about the incident from several different news reports. The third possible witness at 1431 Maple Street, John Wilson, said that he was awake during the time frame of the burglary, but was in the basement doing multiple loads of laundry, making it impossible to see anything outside or hear anything over the sound of the washing machine or drier.

Concise: After securing the burglary scene, I canvassed the area for possible witnesses to the incident. I spoke with the following individuals at their respective addresses: Kent Jones, 1417 Maple Street; Ashley Williams, 1423 Maple Street; and John Wilson, 1431 Maple Street. None of them were in a position to observe or hear anything related to the incident.

Being concise can be summed up simply: Get to the point!

CONSIDERATION OF AUDIENCE

While revising, it is important to keep in mind who will be reading your report. You want to make sure that your report is written at a level that everyone can easily understand. You should write your report such a way that an eighth grader could understand it. There are a few things you can do to be considerate of your audience. Avoid overly complex words. Choose words for their communicative value, not by how fancy they may sound.

This is not an attempt to dumb things down, but a consideration that your audience is merely trying to make your writing universally understandable. Remember the purpose of police reports: to communicate the facts to others in such a manner that they understand what occurred without having been a witness to the occurrence.

Avoid Jargon

Jargon is defined in *Merriam-Webster* (2017) as the technical terminology or characteristic idiom (phrase) of a special activity or group. Jargon may be observed in many different forms and is seldom universally understood by the general public. Jargon includes "10" codes, which are standardized numeric identifiers assigned to replace various commonly used words and phrases. They are most often used by emergency responders to communicate types or characteristics of situations without having to use wordy or time-consuming descriptions (e.g., 10-8 = Available for service, 10-23 = arrived on scene). Unfortunately, such codes, although designed to be standardized, will sometimes vary from jurisdiction to jurisdiction and are very rarely understood by anyone outside of emergency services (police, fire, emergency medical services).

Abbreviations may be another form of jargon (other than those universally understood, such as LASER, SCUBA, D.O.B., aka, vin, SWAT, etc.). Abbreviations such as "perp." for perpetrator, "sus." for suspect, or "vic." for victim, or even "merc." for Mercury or Mercedes or mercenary can cause confusion in the mind of the reader and should be fully articulated as words.

Acronyms, such as PBT for preliminary breath test, ATL for attempt to locate, and GOA for gone on arrival, should be avoided. Such terms should be spelled out completely to ensure that the reader interprets the content of the report properly.

Slang terms, such as "86" for get rid of, "hook" for tow truck, or "tool" for foolish person, cannot be assumed to be understood by the majority of readers and therefore should not be used. Remember, even if local slang is broadly understood by the people in your area, there's no guarantee that at some point an audience outside of your area may be reviewing the report.

CONCLUSION

Officers need to review the first draft of their reports carefully, paying particular attention to the accuracy of their report, as well as how it is put together, to make it understandable, easy to read, and consistent. Officers should understand that during a review, they may find that large portions of their report need to be rewritten. While this process may seem time consuming, it ensures that the report will be of the highest quality. Participating in a process of revising also helps to make officers better writers by highlighting areas in which they need to improve their overall writing skills.

CHAPTER 7

EDITING

COMPETENCY 7: Edit reports for compliance with associated rules of grammar and syntax.

LEARNING OBJECTIVE 1: Recognize improper application of grammar and syntax.
LEARNING OBJECTIVE 2: Apply appropriate grammar and syntax to all sentences within the narrative.

Editing involves adding transitions and fine-tuning language use. This also requires the author to check spelling and punctuation, proofread the report, and check for grammatical and typographical errors. As we have noted throughout the book, officers writing reports need to consider their audience. In this case, officers need to consider that defense attorneys and the media will be reading their reports. If a report has multiple language use errors in the area of spelling and grammar, it makes the reporting officer look ignorant, sloppy, or both. In this chapter we will discuss the editing process and the tools that should initially be used in quality report writing to reduce the need for editing.

Police reports should be written in the "first person," meaning from the writer's point of view, using "I" when referring to self. Following are examples of both incorrect "third-person" and correct "first-person" sentences:

Incorrect: This officer then drew her weapon.
Correct: I then drew my weapon.

Incorrect: Reporting Officer (R/O) then called for a tow truck.
Correct: I then called for a tow truck.

SENTENCE FRAGMENTS/ INCOMPLETE SENTENCES

Communication should be structured in complete sentences. The basic minimal elements of a sentence are a subject and a verb. To be considered a sentence rather than a fragment or a phrase, a group of words must have a subject and a verb. Consider the statement, "The store had been robbed five separate times." Now consider an attempt at the same statement with either the subject or the verb being omitted: "Had been robbed five separate times." This sentence fragment begs the question, "What, or who has been robbed five separate times?" The reason for the follow-up question by the reader is that the sentence fragment lacks a subject and, therefore, the intended message is incomplete and not clearly understood. Think about the statement, "The store had been five separate times." Again, the conveyance of the message is being attempted through the use of a sentence fragment. There is no verb included in the attempted sentence, thereby leading the reader to have to ask the question, "The store had been what five separate times?" Confusion may be compounded if neither a subject nor a verb is included in a statement. Imagine trying to derive meaning from a statement like, "Had been five separate times." So, when checking a report for clarity of communication, review what has been written to ensure that each statement, unless a direct quote, contains the basic elements of a sentence, those being a subject and a verb.

COMPOUND SENTENCES

Compound sentences contain at least two independent clauses joined by a comma, semicolon, or conjunction. Joining the two sentences should help to describe the situation better and make the report easier to read. For example, consider the following two independent clauses: "The subject did not want to fight. He was backed against the wall." In this example, to assist the reader in understanding the thought process behind the subject's actions and to enable the report to flow better, the two independent clauses may be fused with the conjunction "but" to form a compound sentence: "The subject did not want to fight, but he was backed against the wall." The compound sentence communicates to the reader that the subject was caught in a dilemma prior to making a choice or taking action.

RUN-ON SENTENCES

Run-on sentences may typically be observed as one of two varieties: fused sentences and comma splices. A fused sentence occurs when two or more independent clauses are strung together with no marks of punctuation or conjunctions to separate them. For example, the following is a fused sentence: "The witness said that he went over to his girlfriend's house and watched TV for several hours and got in his car to go back home but never made it because a car ran a red light and crashed into his car causing him to have to be taken to the hospital for a head injury that he sustained when his head hit the windshield." This type of run-on sentence may create confusion in the mind of the reader. It wanders from one theme to another without any breaks or transitions to signal a change to the reader. The fused sentence should be separated into multiple independent sentences to keep the progression of events clear. As an alternative to the fused run-on sentence, consider the following sentences: "The witness said that he went over to his girlfriend's house and watched TV for several hours. He then got into his car to go back home, but never made it there because he was involved in an auto accident. A car had run a red light and crashed into his vehicle as he entered the intersection. As a result of the collision, his head struck the windshield of his car causing him injury. He was later transported to the hospital for treatment." By separating the fusion into separate sentences, the sequence of events is easier to follow.

The second type of run-on sentence, a comma splice, occurs when the writer splices multiple clauses into one sentence through overuse of commas. The following represents a version of the previous example in the form of a comma splice: "The witness said he went over to his girlfriend's house, watched TV for several hours, got into his car to go home, never made it because a car ran a red light and crashed into his car, he hit his head on the windshield and he had to be taken to the hospital to be treated for a head injury." Just as in the case of the fused, run-on sentence, it will be much easier for the reader to understand the sequence of events if the comma splice is separated into separate sentences similar to the ones noted above.

WORD USAGE (HOMOPHONES)

Homophones are words that sound the same but have different meanings. Common homophones include *there, their, they're; bye, by, buy; four, for, fore; hear, here; know, no; male, mail; pare, pear, pair; to, two, too; wear, where; bare, bear*. Imagine attempting to communicate one idea using a word that creates an entirely different image. For example, explaining that someone crossed the gravel driveway in bear feet is entirely different than describing someone who crossed a gravel driveway in bare feet. The first statement implies that the person crossing the gravel driveway had the feet of a bear, which is quite impossible. The second statement tells the reader that the person who crossed the gravel driveway was wearing no shoes or socks. Frequently, the words *there, their,* and *they're* are used interchangeably. The meaning of each is quite distinct. The word *there* refers to a location. The word *their* is a plural, third-person, possessive pronoun used to associate persons with possessions, ideas, or other people. The word *they're* is a contraction of the words *they* and *are*. Identification of each word with its definition makes it easy to see how the misapplication of a word alters the message being sent, thereby creating inaccuracies and confusion, two conditions that should never be generated by police reports.

On this point, be sure not to rely on spellcheck to check correct usage. Computer programs, though helpful, can fail to recognize the context of a sentence and recommend an incorrect word. Also, please realize that it will not recognize typographical errors that are correctly spelled words. For instance, if you meant to type "for" and you type "fro" instead, spellcheck will not catch this error because "fro" is a word. Please be sure to spellcheck your report; spelling accuracy is important. However, be sure to monitor the context of suggested changes so that your report contains the correct words. Finally, read your report over word-for-word to ensure that spellcheck did not fail to catch a misspelled word.

USE OF PERSONAL PRONOUNS *I* AND *ME*

A frequent occurrence in both police report writing and oral communication is use of the word *myself* in the place of *I* or *me*. Read the following sentences and observe how awkward each sentence sounds.

> Give it to *myself* no later than Friday. (me)
> Suspect Doe tried to escape from Officer Brown and *myself*. (me)
> Smith and *myself* then returned to the squad car. (I)
> Officer Brown and *myself* were the first to arrive. (I)

Now try reading the same sentences using the appropriate pronoun shown in the parenthesis at the end of each sentence. The sentences should sound and flow better in the mind of the reader when the appropriate pronoun is applied.

Many struggle with the decision about when to use *I* or *me*. Consider the following sentence: "John and me went to the store." This is actually an improper sentence. It should state, "John and I went to the store." The test of which first-person pronoun to use would be to eliminate the reference to the other person in the sentence. The first, improper sentence would then read, "Me went to the store." The improper usage of the first-person pronoun becomes immediately apparent. Conversely, in consideration of the second sentence, "I went to the store," it becomes clear that the appropriate pronoun has been used.

Now consider this sentence: "The witness made the statement to Detective Davis and I." Again, this is an improper sentence. It should be stated, "The witness made the statement to Detective Davis and me." By taking "Detective Davis" out of the sentence, the appropriate first-person pronoun usage becomes clear. "The witness made the statement to me," not "The witness made the statement to I."

PRONOUN AGREEMENT

If a subject of a sentence is singular, the pronoun must also be singular. If the subject is plural, the pronoun must also be plural. For example, if a sentence is initiated by talking about the actions of a singular suspect, the description of those actions should be described as "his" or "hers," not "theirs" or "their," which applies to the actions of multiple people. The word *his* or *hers* applies to the actions of a singular person.

Wrong: The subject was seen on video using their hands to pry open the door.
Correct: The subject was seen on video using his hands to pry open the door.

USE OF PRONOUNS VS. PROPER NOUNS

When documenting the statements of someone else, summarizing a witness statement for example, an officer should avoid excessive use of expressions such as "he said," "he stated," "the speaker added," "the speaker then went on to say," "the subject also thinks," and so on. You should also avoid solely using the subject's name. Instead, consider alternating between using the subject's name and using a pronoun every other sentence when possible. Consider the following examples.

Solely using subject's name: "I spoke with Jessica Smith, a witness to the altercation. Smith stated that Smith had seen some minor pushing between Jones and Davis. Smith said that neither of the subjects appeared to be injured by the pushing. Smith said that Smith was going to take her sister Jones with her to Springfield for the night so that the situation could de-escalate."

This example is hard to read due to the repetition of the word "Smith." It does not flow well.

Overuse of pronouns: "I spoke with Jessica Smith, a witness to the altercation. She stated that she had seen some minor pushing between Jones and Davis. She said that neither of the subjects appeared to be injured by the pushing. She said that she was going to take her sister Jones with her to Springfield for the night so that the situation could de-escalate."

This example is hard to read due to the repetition of the word "she," as well as the possible confusion over who the word "she" is referring to. Consequently, it does not flow well either.

Combination example: "I spoke with Jessica Smith, a witness to the altercation. Smith stated that she had seen some minor pushing between Jones and Davis. She said that neither of the subjects appeared to be injured by the pushing. Smith said that she was going to take her sister Jones with her to Springfield for the night so that the situation could de-escalate."

In this case, the officer is not repeating the name "Smith" in every sentence, but using it enough that it is clear who the pronoun "she" is referring to.

WRITE IN THE PAST TENSE

When editing, be sure to pay close attention that your writing does not mix past and present tenses. Generally, police reports are written in past tense, but be sure to follow your agency policy on this point. Whichever tense the writer chooses, he or she should use it throughout.

Examples of tense confusion:

Wrong: Then John calls me back, since he was not in when I called him.
Correct: Then John called me back, since he was not in when I called him.

Wrong: She waited as I finished writing. I then go back to her car and explain the citation to her. (went, explained)
Correct: She waited as I finished writing. I then went back to her car and explained the citation to her.

Shifting from one tense to the other creates an impression of uncertainty. When writing a police report, an officer should always use past tense. All of the actions and events you will be writing about will have occurred in the past, so you can feel safe writing in the past tense. The only exception to this rule is when there is anticipated action, such as follow-up. For example, "I will interview SMITH when he returns to town next week."

CONCISENESS

Good writing is concise, that is, brief yet comprehensive. You should avoid unnecessary use of adjectives or using useless adjectives. Obviously, using adjectives to describe things is important to your writing, for instance: "The striking vehicle was yellow." However, those adjectives must have meaning and be useful to the sentence. Words like "really," "incredibly," and "huge" are abstract and do not actually make any useful observations in a police report.

For example:

Wrong: JONES had a really big cut on his face.
Correct: JONES had a 4-inch cut on his face.

Wrong: There was a huge dent in the front fender of the victim's vehicle.
Correct: There was an 18-inch-diameter dent in the front fender of the victim's vehicle.

Wrong: DAVIS raised his fist in a belligerent manner.
Correct: DAVIS clenched his fist, assumed a boxer stance, and rolled his shoulders forward toward me as if preparing to attack.

USE OF APPROPRIATE LEVEL OF DETAIL

Pay careful attention to the final example above. Note that the "correct" sentence is longer than the "wrong" sentence. This would appear to violate the rule of being concise. However, the "wrong" sentence is completely devoid of objective detail. It uses the subjective adjective *belligerent* to describe what should be an objective action (being assaulted). It begs the question: "What does belligerent mean?" It is the reporting officer's opinion based on the situation he or she observed. Officers should use detailed observations and factual statements rather than stating their opinion. The second sentence describes that in detail, in this case providing justification for a use of force. A general guideline in these cases is to use concrete language instead of abstract language.

Some common examples:

Wrong: The subject's behavior was suspicious.
Correct: At 3:00 am, I saw the subject peering into the jewelry store window. He quickly ducked into the shadows as I approached.

Wrong: There were a number of deep scratches in the door of the car.
Correct: There were 12 scratches down to the primer coat in the door of the car.

Wrong: My RADAR unit indicated the vehicle was moving at a high rate of speed.
Correct: My RADAR unit indicated the vehicle was moving 75 mph.

Wrong: JONES reported that SMITH used abusive language.
Correct: JONES reported that SMITH called her a "fat bitch."

AVOIDING AMBIGUITY

In addition to using appropriate detail while being concise, officers need to make sure their words unambiguously describe the incident. Words are subject to interpretation. A good report writer works to ensure that there are as few interpretations that can be drawn from a statement as possible. Great care should be taken to ensure that statements recorded in a report reflect the facts as observed and do not lend themselves to erroneous interpretation. Consider the following statements:

Ambiguous: The suspect came out of the window with a TV as I watched it.
Unambiguous: As I watched the window, the suspect emerged with a TV.

Ambiguous: I noticed it was red as the car went through the light.
Unambiguous: I noticed the light was red as the car went through the intersection without stopping.

Ambiguous: Why did you take the money the victim said they asked.
Unambiguous: The victim said that the suspects asked, "Why did you take the money?"

Ambiguous: The witnesses told me exactly what I saw.
Unambiguous: The witnesses' statements confirmed my observations.

Being concise does not require an officer to make all sentences short. Nor does the officer have to avoid all adjectives. Officers need to make every word count; every word should help to tell the narrative story.

USE OF OFFICIOUS WORDS

In Chapter 6, we discussed avoiding jargon. Similar to that concept is avoiding the use of officious words, that is, using certain words to make your report sound more official. The word *in* is an example that can make your report sound officious, as in the phrase "in color." In addition, using such words violates the principle of being concise, and is not grammatically correct. Examples:

Wrong: I did respond to the call at 0300 hours.
Correct: I responded to the call at 0300 hours.

Wrong: The sergeant did tell me that he would attend the meeting.
Correct: The sergeant told me that he would attend the meeting.

Wrong: The striking vehicle was yellow in color.
Correct: The striking vehicle was yellow.

Officers should also make an effort to use everyday words. For example:

Wrong: I observed the subject vehicle drive over the sidewalk.
Correct: I saw the subject vehicle drive over the sidewalk.

Wrong: I then proceeded to jail with JONES.
Correct: I then went to jail with JONES. Or, phrased better: I then transported JONES to jail.

Wrong: SMITH indicated JONES hit her.
Correct: SMITH said JONES hit her.

Wrong: I initiated contact with the subject.
Correct: I asked the subject to speak with me.

AVOIDING USE OF AN INFORMAL TONE

Although you should use everyday words to avoid sounding officious, you should avoid adopting an informal tone in your writing. You have your own way of speaking when you are in a conversation with your friends, family, and coworkers. This may not always be grammatically correct, but it is acceptable because you are "among friends." You should, however, strive to avoid using an informal tone in your writing. As noted in Chapter 6, you have to consider your audience and what your writing style tells them about you. There are certain improper uses of the English language that are tolerated in everyday, informal conversations, that if used in a police report will misrepresent you as unprofessional or uneducated. For example:

Wrong: I seen a white juvenile male run out of the store.
Correct: I saw a white juvenile male run out of the store.

Wrong: So I says to him, "Stop right there. Police!"
Correct: I said to him, "Stop right there. Police!"

Wrong: He goes, "Keep your hands off me."
Correct: He said, "Keep your hands off me."

On this point, remember that your police report will be reviewed by prosecutors and defense attorneys when they are preparing their cases, as well as any future appeals.

USE OF TRANSITIONAL WORDS AND PHRASES

Most of your reports will be longer than one paragraph. It will be important that you are able to tie your paragraphs together into a cohesive police report. Sometimes you will need to express that two or more paragraphs are linked, to improve the flow of your report and help readers to understand it better. Sometimes this will involve the use of an entire sentence, but usually you will be able to do this with a simple word or phrase, such as:

First	*Second*	*Third*
Next	*Then*	*Initially*
Later	*Additionally*	*Furthermore*
Finally	*Last*	*In conclusion*

CONCLUSION

Editing is an important part of your report writing process. It gives you another opportunity to read through your report and ensure that there are no factual errors or omissions. Just as importantly, it allows you to craft your report into a fully professional document. Remember, you always need to consider your audience when you are writing. The audience for your report will invariably include entities outside of your department, including media and defense attorneys. As a professional, you do not want to look amateurish, especially to those outside of your department who may use an unprofessional report to diminish your credibility. Therefore, take the time to carefully read through and edit your report before submitting it.

CHAPTER 8

SUBMITTING AND AFTER-SUBMISSION CONCERNS

COMPETENCY 8: Perform final review prior to report submission.

LEARNING OBJECTIVE 1: Proofread report for adherence to fundamental concepts of

COMPETENCY 9: Develop a supplemental narrative report.

LEARNING OBJECTIVE 1: Identify information that should be included in a supplemental narrative report.

COMPETENCY 10: Dispose of field notes appropriately.

LEARNING OBJECTIVE 1: Identify associated policies regarding retention/disposal of field notes.
LEARNING OBJECTIVE 2: Articulate preservation of field notes within report when applicable.

Once the process of editing is complete, you may feel like you have reached the end of a long race. Sometimes wearily, you will be ready to submit your report, if for no other reason than to just get it off your desk. Remember that this is the end of a long process, and you would not want to make a mistake so late in the race. This chapter will review some concerns about the submission process, as well as some concerns to bear in mind after submitting your report, such as requests for revision, supplemental information, and retention of field notes.

FINAL CHECK

After revising, but prior to submitting, read your report one last time. Read the entire report. If possible, read it aloud. This will give you an idea of what the report sounds like to someone else. Remember that just because something you wrote makes sense to you, it may not make sense to someone else who does not have the same level of intimate knowledge of the case as you (as in the example from Chapter 7: *The suspect came out of the window with a TV as I watched it*).

In many cases, once your report is submitted, it becomes part of the public record. Once a part of the public record, any changes you make to your report will be able to be compared to previous versions of the report. These changes will be subject to review by other interested parties to the case, such as defense attorneys, and potentially used to cast doubt on the accuracy of your report.

REQUESTS FOR REVISION

Although changes to a report are subject to review, that is not to say that you will be absolutely unable to revise your report after submitting it. Requests for revision may come from a reviewing supervisor or a transcriptionist. In such cases, corrections should be made in a timely manner and the report should be resubmitted as quickly as possible. Chances are, there are people waiting to access your report. Keep in mind, once your original report has been altered, your revision may be labeled by the agency as having been "amended." This should not be cause for alarm, but in the event that the report is referenced in a court proceeding, it may be necessary for you to explain why the report has been amended.

Short of a directive of a supervisor or the transcriptionists, or your own discovery of an error, reports should not be amended. There may be times when interested third parties (insurance adjusters, attorneys, business owners, etc.) contact you in an attempt to have a report revised to more closely match their perception or recollection of events. You are the fact finder, so any information that you have included in your report should remain unaltered, despite requests of anyone other than authorized personnel.

SUPPLEMENTAL INFORMATION

Frequently, additional information about a specific incident, event, or investigation surfaces. Such information may include but is not limited to evidence, findings of another investigator, late statements, discrepancies between witness accounts, or other new information. In each case, as stated previously, altering the original report will not be an option. Therefore, a supplemental report, capturing new information, should be submitted at the time that such information is discovered.

WHAT TO DO WITH FIELD NOTES

Depending on your jurisdiction, your field notes may be considered a public record. In these cases, field notes represent long-term documentation which may be used as evidence at trial and they may be used to refresh your memory while testifying. Accurate and complete field notes can be a valuable aid in ensuring the admissibility of evidence related to a crime scene (WI DOJ, 2014). Officers that are required to retain their notes as a public record should follow all relevant department policies and state laws regarding record retention.

Officers who are not subject to retaining their field notes must consider carefully what they will do with their notes after completing their report. In these cases, many officers opt to shred their notes after the report has been drafted. While allowable, it removes the opportunity for the officer to refer to his notes in the future.

On the other hand, it may be tempting to officers to retain their notes at home or in their locker for their future reference. In this case, officers will have their reports and field notes available at trial. However, officers must guard their notes carefully, as they will invariably contain personally identifying information of the suspects, victims, and witnesses they have interviewed. This personally identifying information, in the wrong hands, would provide a ripe opportunity for identity theft. Additionally, if a defense attorney ascertains that an officer keeps the field notes, he or she will be able to subpoena those notes for review and possibly use them at trial. This places officers in the same situation as officers forced to retain their records, except that the department will have no policy on which notes to deliver and which not. In these cases, it is important for officers to file a request with the court that limits the subpoena's reach to only those records pertaining to the matter at hand.

For all of these reasons, in the absence of state law and agency policy regarding the retention of field notes, it may be advisable to destroy the notes to avoid their use as a means to reveal inconsistencies (whether actual or perceived) between their contents and those of the official report. If you are a member of an agency that requires retention of field notes, if field notes had been written in a notebook containing multiple days or even months' worth of notes, a responsible officer should request of the court the restriction of attorney access to only the notes pertinent to the event in question. This will prevent attorneys from embarking on a "fishing expedition" to discover characteristics of officer note-taking that they may attempt to use to diminish the credibility of the officer.

CONCLUSION

Throughout the previous chapters, we have discussed foundational aspects of basic police report writing. At the beginning of your career, development of quality reports may require considerable concentration. As a new officer gains experience in writing quality reports, inclusion of these foundational aspects will become second nature. Regardless of level of experience, however, officers should never lose focus of their attention to detail in every aspect of their job performance, particularly with respect to police report writing. In the next section we will be introducing a number of practical exercises geared toward the completion of a variety of commonly used police reports and the development of fundamental police report writing skills.

PART II
PRACTICAL EXERCISES

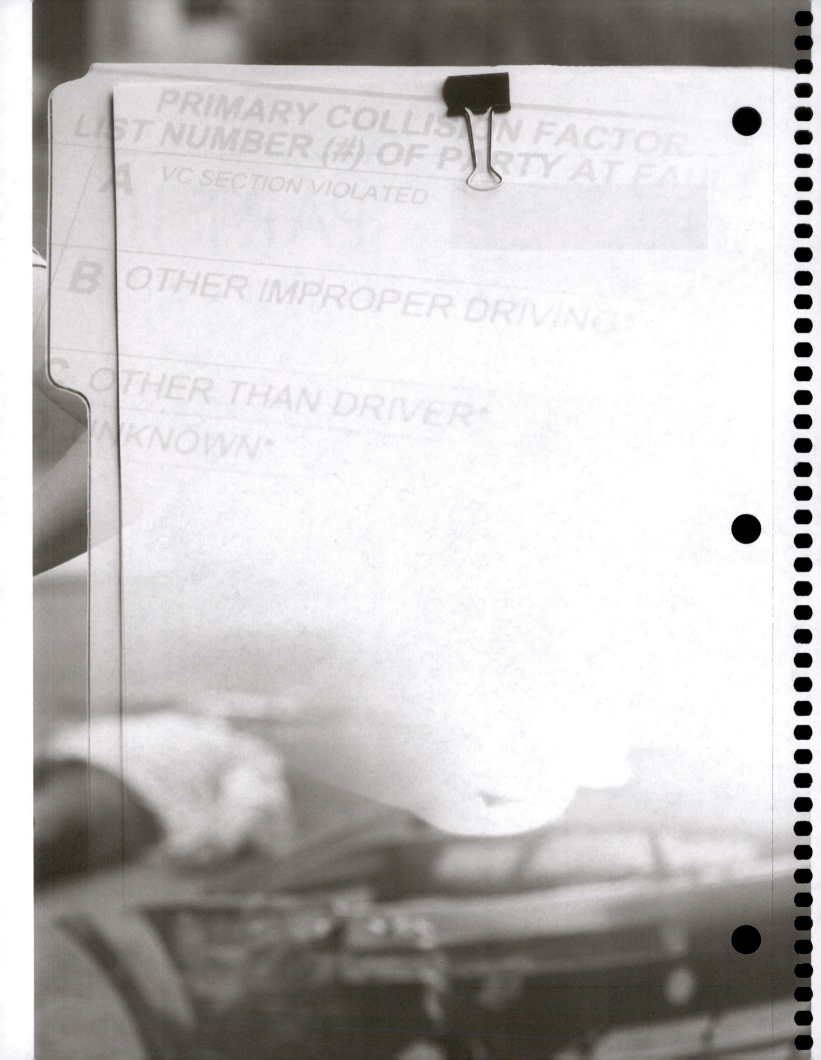

PRIMARY COLLISION FACTOR.

LIST NUMBER (#) OF PARTY AT FAULT

A. VC SECTION VIOLATED.

B. OTHER IMPROPER DRIVING.

OTHER THAN DRIVER*

UNKNOWN*

COMPLETION OF CITIZEN CONTACT (FIELD INTERVIEW)

Instructions: Complete a Citizen Contact (Field Interview) (located below) based on the following scenario.

Scenario: You are working for the Appleton Police Department as a uniformed patrol officer. Your officer number is 5613. You are assigned to the second shift (4 pm to midnight) on Sqd. 46R. At approximately 4:15 pm, you are dispatched to see the complainant, Carlton J. Post, white / male, DOB: 07-11-47, of 811 N. 5th St., Appleton, WI, Ph. 920-277-0352, regarding a suspicious person who has been sitting outside of the tavern across the street from Post's house for the past hour. You arrive at 4:20 pm and talk to Post who says that he just thought it was strange that the person had been sitting there for the past hour. You tell Post that you will check the situation out.

At approximately 4:23 pm you cross the street and approach a young man who is sitting on the sidewalk in front of Wally Gator's Tavern, 818 N. 5th St, with his back to the street, using a telephone pole as a back rest. He identifies himself as Bradley C. Cambridge, white / male, DOB: 10-30-96, of 4738 Cordona Lane, Menasha, WI 54310, Ph. (920)773-8310. After introducing yourself and explaining the reason for the contact, you ask Cambridge why he has been sitting there for the past hour. He is cooperative and explains that his uncle, Roger Cambridge, is the owner of the tavern. Bradley goes on to say that he is employed by his uncle and cleans the tavern every day before it opens at 8 pm. He tells you that he had a key for the tavern, but he lost it on the way to work today. Bradley says that he called his uncle who is on his way from New London to come open up the tavern so that it can be cleaned. Bradley tells you that he had just been waiting for his uncle to arrive. Roger Cambridge has a cell phone number of (920)323-1499.

After confirming Bradley's identity and story, you recontact Post to let him know what you have discovered. You then use your field notes to complete a Citizen Contact (Field Interview) report of your contact with Bradley.

CITIZEN CONTACT REPORT

BLANK FORM (TOP)

CITIZEN CONTACT REPORT			INCIDENT NO.		OFFENSE REPORT	Y ☐ N ☐
					JUVENILE	Y ☐ N ☐
NAME - LAST	FIRST	MIDDLE	AKA/NICKNAME		SCHOOL	GRADE
ADDRESS		CITY, STATE, ZIP	PHONE			

TYPE OF CONTACT

☐ 1 WARNING: City Ordinance Violation. Failure to correct or comply can result in legal action being commenced against you.

☐ 2 WARNING: Vehicle Traffic Law Violation. You have violated a traffic law that is described in the narrative section of this notice.

☐ 3 VEHICLE DEFECT: The violation(s) indicated must be corrected at once. ALL FUTURE OPERATIONS WITHOUT CORRECTION ARE ILLEGAL.

☐ 4 BICYCLE VIOLATION

☐ 5 FIELD INTERROGATION

☐ 6 REPORT IN PERSON: Report to the Police Department

☐ 7 OTHER CONTACT

☐ Within 15 days sign this notice and mail or bring it to the _____ Police Department, unless you are instructed to report in person. FAILURE TO COMPLY CAN RESULT IN ARREST ACTION AGAINST YOU.

I CERTIFY THAT THE LISTED VIOLATION(S) HAVE BEEN CORRECTED:

DEPARTMENT COPY

COMPLETED FORM (BOTTOM)

CITIZEN CONTACT REPORT			INCIDENT NO. 00-000-00		OFFENSE REPORT	Y ☐ N ☒
					JUVENILE	Y ☐ N ☒
NAME - LAST: Rupiper,	FIRST: Brian	MIDDLE: X.	AKA/NICKNAME: "Pipe"		SCHOOL	GRADE

ADDRESS: 7453 Union Grove Dr. CITY, STATE, ZIP: Mayville WI 57163 PHONE: 920-984-5553

BIRTHDATE	M	F	WHI.	BLK.	NAT.AM.	ASN.	HISP.	HEIGHT	WEIGHT	HAIR	EYES
08-04-80	☒	☐	☒	☐	☐	☐	☐	6'1"	180	BRO	BLU

SCARS, MARKS, TATTOOS LOCATIONS/DESCRIPTION: Tattoo of "Pipe" L. Upper Arm   PARENTS: Deceased

DRIVER'S LICENSE: R000-6152-0404-02 STATE: WI EXP.: 09 SOCIAL SECURITY #: 393-72-3142 PROB./PAR. Y ☐ N ☒

VEH. PLATE/VIN: PYP MAN EXP.: 03 STATE: WI MAKE: Ford YEAR: 1999 MODEL: 2dr COLOR: SIL

DATE OF OFFENSE: 08-18-02 TIME: 0300 LOCATION OF OFFENSE: 417 Commercial Way

CONTACT NARRATIVE: I saw Rupiper looking in a jewelry store window with a flashlight. He ducked into the shadows as I approached

SIGNATURE OF CONTACTED PERSON: Brian Rupiper OFFICER SIGNATURE: P.O. Joe Williams OFFICER NO.: 5617

GANG INFO - GANG NAME STATUS MEMBER ☐ ASSOCIATE ☐ SUSPECTED ☐ GANG MEMBER ID CRITERIA 1 2 3 4 5 6 7 8 CIRCLE APPLICABLE NUMBERS

ASSOCIATES BIRTHDATE ADDRESS PHONE
1)
2)

TYPE OF CONTACT

☐ 1 WARNING: City Ordinance Violation. Failure to correct or comply can result in legal action being commenced against you.

☐ 2 WARNING: Vehicle Traffic Law Violation. You have violated a traffic law that is described in the narrative section of this notice.

☐ 3 VEHICLE DEFECT: The violation(s) indicated must be corrected at once. ALL FUTURE OPERATIONS WITHOUT CORRECTION ARE ILLEGAL.

☐ 4 BICYCLE VIOLATION

☒ 5 FIELD INTERROGATION

☐ 6 REPORT IN PERSON: Report to the Police Department

☐ 7 OTHER CONTACT

☐ Within 15 days sign this notice and mail or bring it to the _____ Police Department, unless you are instructed to report in person. FAILURE TO COMPLY CAN RESULT IN ARREST ACTION AGAINST YOU.

I CERTIFY THAT THE LISTED VIOLATION(S) HAVE BEEN CORRECTED:

SIGNATURE CERTIFICATION DATE

DEPARTMENT COPY

POLICE REPORT WRITING
Exercise 1
Citizen Contact (Field Interview)

RUBRIC

Requirement	Learner		Instructor	
	Included	Not Included	Included	Not Included
Student has reviewed the associated assignment scenario.				
Associated Competency **CO 2:** Differentiate reports based on type and purpose.				
Dispatch time, nature of the assignment, address of the assignment, arrival and back-in-service times have been recorded in student's field notes.				
Associated Competency **CO 4:** Construct a narrative report in a chronological format.				
Student has gathered information from the reporting party/complainant and recorded it in his or her field notes.				
Associated Competency **CO 3:** Demonstrate thorough preparation to develop a report.				
Student has gathered information from the subject of the field interview and recorded it in his or her field notes.				
Associated Competency **CO 3:** Demonstrate thorough preparation to develop a report.				
Student has recorded the disposition/resolution of this call in his or her field notes.				
Associated Competency **CO 4:** Construct a narrative report in a chronological format.				

Student has analyzed the situation as well as the information gathered and has arrived at a course of action that will result in an appropriate resolution.				
Student has determined whether a crime or ordinance violation has occurred.				
Student has concluded that a Citizen Contact Report is suitable and appropriate for the situation presented in the scenario.				
Student has utilized information collected throughout the contact to confirm statements and to arrive at a resolution.				
Associated Competency **CO 3**: Demonstrate thorough preparation to develop a report.				
All applicable fields of the Citizen Contact form have been completed by the student.				
The report is clear, legible, and free of errors or stray marks.				
The report evidences correct grammar, punctuation, and spelling.				
Associated Competency **CO 7:** Edit reports for compliance with associated rules of grammar and syntax.				
Learner has ensured that all elements of the rubric have been fulfilled and the deadline for this report has been met.				

FOUND PROPERTY

Instructions: Complete a Citizen Contact (Field Interview) (located below) based on the following scenario.

On September 25, 2018, while in your squad car, writing the narrative for a recently issued traffic citation, you are approached by a boy who claims that he just found some fireworks in the doorway of an abandoned, Badger Materials warehouse. The fireworks consisted of 10 Black Cat firecrackers, 14 Sky Blaster bottle rockets, 2 Emperor's Choice roman candles, and 12 Independence Day sparklers. The boy said that he and a friend were walking home from school and found the fireworks. He said that he knew they were illegal because, last summer, his cousin got a ticket from the police for "blowing off" fireworks. He said that, after discovering the fireworks, he then saw the police and didn't want to get in trouble. That's when he decided to give the fireworks to you. He then asks you if he can keep them if no one else comes to claim them.

Incident report #18-00579-416

Your location when the boy approached you: 127 W. 9th St.

You are assigned to Green Bay Police Squad 16A

Location of the warehouse: 225 W. 7th St., Green Bay, Outagamie County, WI (east doorway)

Time that you were approached by the boy: 3:45 pm

Inventory # 7734129

Boy who discovered the fireworks: Adam K. Larkin, White / Male, DOB: 03-31-2003, 1819 Summit Circle, Green Bay, WI 54307, Ph. (920)843-1639

Second boy: Anthony M. Finch, DOB: 09-14-2002, 447 W. 9th St., Green Bay, WI 54307, Ph. (920)843-2165

INCIDENT REPORT

Date:_____   Incident #_____

Nature of Incident:_____

Complainant:_____

Suspect:_____

Victim:_____

Witness #1:_____

Witness #2:_____

Witness #3:_____

Narrative:

_____

_____

_____

_____

_____

_____

_____

_____

_____

_____

_____

_____

_____

_____

_____

_____

_____

_____

Officer Signature _____

Officer Printed Name _____ Badge Number _____

POLICE REPORT WRITING
Exercise 2
Citizen Contact (Found Property Narrative)

RUBRIC

Requirement	Learner		Instructor	
	Included	Not Included	Included	Not Included
Student has reviewed the associated assignment scenario.				
Associated Competency **CO 2:** Differentiate reports based on type and purpose.				
Dispatch time, nature of the assignment, address of the assignment, arrival and back-in-service times have been recorded in student's field notes.				
Associated Competency **CO 4:** Construct a narrative report in a chronological format.				
Student has gathered information from the reporting party/complainant and recorded it in his or her field notes.				
Student has recorded the disposition/resolution of this call in his or her field notes.				
Associated Competency **CO 3:** Demonstrate thorough preparation to develop a report.				
Student has analyzed the situation as well as the information gathered and has arrived at a course of action that will result in an appropriate resolution.				
Student has determined whether a crime or ordinance violation has occurred.				
Student has documented details such as times, locations, incident #, inventory #, description of property to include brand names throughout the narrative report.				

Associated Competency **CO 4:** Construct a narrative report in a chronological format.				
Student has utilized information collected throughout the contact to confirm statements and to arrive at a resolution.				
Report contains an "<u>Introduction</u>" paragraph as well as an "<u>Investigation</u>" paragraph and a "<u>Disposition</u>" paragraph.				
Associated Competency **CO 4:** Construct a narrative report in a chronological format.				
The report is clear, legible, and free of errors or stray marks.				
The report evidences correct grammar, punctuation, and spelling.				
Associated Competency **CO 7:** Edit reports for compliance with associated rules of grammar and syntax.				
Learner has ensured that all elements of the rubric have been fulfilled and the deadline for this report has been met.				

EXERCISE 3

DAMAGE TO SQUAD

Instructions: Using a standard narrative format (Introduction, Body, Conclusion) construct a complete and detailed squad damage report based on the following scenario.

Scenario: On Tuesday, September 18, 2018, at 7:30 pm, you go to the garage and sign out vehicle 819. Vehicle 819 is a marked, 2015, Dodge, Charger, 4 door, bearing WI 446273 "Official-LE" registration plates. In accordance with your agency policy, you inspect the vehicle prior to going into service. During that inspection, you discover a large dent (approximately the size of a bowling ball) in the right rear quarter panel, between the wheel well and the end of the bumper area. The officers from the previous shift are still inside the garage unloading equipment. You approach Officer Randy Powell who had just signed vehicle 819 in at the end of his shift. You ask him if he had reported the damage to the vehicle and, looking puzzled, he asks what you are talking about. You both go out to look at the dent and, upon seeing it, Officer Powell said that he'd never seen the dent before and that it was not there at the beginning of his shift at 7:30 am. You then suggest to Powell that one of you needs to tell a supervisor about the damage. Officer Powell insists that it was not there at the beginning of his shift, nor did it occur at any time throughout his shift. He tells you that since you are the one who discovered the damage, you should be the one to notify the supervisor about it. You then go back into the station and talk to Sgt. Vitali who accompanies you back to the vehicle to inspect the damage. He asks you who had driven the vehicle previously and if you had talked to that officer. You acknowledge that it was Officer Powell and that you have already spoken to Powell about the damage. You share Powell's response with Sgt. Vitali who informs you that, because of the extent of the damage, you will have to write a detailed report documenting it. Incident # 18-79252-672.

INCIDENT REPORT

Date:_____   Incident #_____

Nature of Incident:_____

Complainant:_____

Suspect:_____

Victim:_____

Witness #1:_____

Witness #2:_____

Witness #3:_____

Narrative:

_____

_____

_____

_____

_____

_____

_____

_____

_____

_____

_____

_____

_____

_____

_____

_____

_____

Officer Signature _____

Officer Printed Name _____ Badge Number _____

POLICE REPORT WRITING
Exercise 3
Damage to Squad-Report Narrative

RUBRIC

Requirement	Learner		Instructor	
	Included	Not Included	Included	Not Included
Student has reviewed the associated assignment scenario.				
Associated Competency **CO 2:** Differentiate reports based on type and purpose.				
Squad and shift assignment have been recorded in student's field notes.				
Time of discovery and details of damage have been recorded in student's field notes.				
Vehicle information has been recorded in student's field notes.				
Student has recorded any other related information in his or her field notes.				
Time and location of supervisory notification is recorded in student's field notes.				
Associated Competency **CO 3:** Demonstrate thorough preparation to develop a report.				
Student has documented the time of discovery, information gathering, and reporting of squad damage in a narrative report.				
Narrative contains detailed descriptions of the vehicle and the damage.				

Narrative documents statements and actions of other officers/ supervisor regarding this incident.				
Report contains an "Introduction" paragraph as well as an "Investigation" paragraph and a "Disposition" paragraph.				
Associated Competency **CO 4:** Construct a narrative report in a chronological format.				
The report is clear, legible, and free of errors or stray marks.				
The report evidences correct grammar, punctuation, and spelling.				
Associated Competency **CO 7:** Edit reports for compliance with associated rules of grammar and syntax.				
Learner has ensured that all elements of the rubric have been fulfilled and the deadline for this report has been met.				

EXERCISE 4

BURGLARY ALARM

Scenario: On August 28, 2018, at 11:27 pm, you are called to respond to Jackson's Garage, 164 Matthews Street for a burglary alarm. Dispatch advises you that it is a front door alarm. Officer Vega notified dispatch that he will be en route to back you up.

Upon arrival, you find the front door locked, and no lights appear to be on inside the building. You request that dispatch notify a keyholder to meet you at the scene. You check the perimeter and find the rest of the building to be secure, with no indications that anyone has broken in. While awaiting the keyholder/owner, you post backup officers at opposing corners of the building to maintain the perimeter while you and officer Vega check the inside of the building. At 11:45 pm, the business owner Evan Jackson (White / Male, DOB: 11-19-1969, 92 Ripple Street, Ph. 920-715-5190) arrives on scene. He unlocks the front door for you and Vega to enter. You search the building for suspects and/or evidence of a crime, finding that nothing appears out of order. Jackson then checks the building, telling you afterward that everything appears in order. Jackson then secures the front door, and you go back in service.

Instructions: Complete a report detailing how you handled the call (from beginning to end). Incident # 18-24097-284.

Field notes must be taken to gather the following information (at a minimum):

- Time of dispatch
- Initial observations (e.g., cars in parking lot or leaving the area, open doors, lights)
- Immediate actions (e.g., perimeter, checking doors)
- If contact, complete information on keyholder
- Clearing of building: note anything out of order
- Securing of building
- Arrival time
- Squad number
- Backup officers, as well as their role at the scene and where they were positioned
- Keyholder's arrival time must be documented and he or she must be identified and checked.
- How the building was secured should also be documented.

INCIDENT REPORT

Date:_____   Incident #_____

Nature of Incident:_____

Complainant:_____

Suspect:_____

Victim:_____

Witness #1:_____

Witness #2:_____

Witness #3:_____

Narrative:

_____

_____

_____

_____

_____

_____

_____

_____

_____

_____

_____

_____

_____

_____

_____

_____

_____

Officer Signature _____

Officer Printed Name _____ Badge Number _____

POLICE REPORT WRITING
Exercise 4
Burglary Alarm Report Narrative

RUBRIC

Requirement	Learner		Instructor	
	Included	Not Included	Included	Not Included
Student has reviewed the assignment scenarios.				
Associated Competency **CO 2:** Differentiate reports based on type and purpose.				
Squad and shift assignment have been recorded in student's field notes.				
Time of dispatch and nature of assignment have been recorded in student's field notes.				
Observations of the scene (upon arrival and throughout investigation) have been recorded in student's field notes.				
Name of keyholder has been recorded in student's field notes.				
Student has recorded any other related information in his or her field notes (Incident #, Sqd #s and last names of assisting officers, backup arrival times, etc.).				
Time and location of supervisory notification is recorded in student's field notes.				
Associated Competency **CO 3:** Demonstrate thorough preparation to develop a report.				
Student has documented his or her response to this assignment from beginning to end.				

Squad and shift assignment have been recorded in student's report narrative.				
Time of dispatch and nature of assignment have been recorded in student's report narrative.				
Observations of the scene (upon arrival and throughout investigation) have been recorded in student's report narrative.				
Narrative contains detailed, chronological descriptions of officer actions and observations.				
Narrative documents statements and actions of other officers/supervisor, witnesses, suspects, keyholders, etc., regarding this incident (Incident #, Sqd #s and last names of assisting officers, backup arrival times, physical descriptions, etc. have been included in the narrative).				
Name of keyholder/bank representative has been recorded in student's report narrative.				
Report contains an "Introduction" paragraph as well as an "Investigation" paragraph and a "Disposition" paragraph.				
Associated Competency **CO 4:** Construct a narrative report in a chronological format.				
The report is clear, legible, and free of errors or stray marks.				
The report evidences correct grammar, punctuation, and spelling.				
Associated Competency **CO 7:** Edit reports for compliance with associated rules of grammar and syntax.				
Learner has ensured that all elements of the rubric have been fulfilled and the deadline for this report has been met.				

EXERCISE 5

CRIMINAL DAMAGE TO PROPERTY

Instructions: Upon completion of your field notes, write a detailed offense report documenting what was reported and the details of your investigation.

On March 3, 2018, at 7:50 am, you are called to respond to Bob's Market, 1403 E. Ramsey St. for the complaint of Damage to Property (Incident # 18-48751-332). Upon arrival, you are met by the store owner who was also the clerk/victim Robert S. Mattingly, white / male, DOB 5-17-1960, 4512 N. 19th St., Appleton, WI 54911, Ph. (920)882-3311. You meet with him outside the front door of the store. Looking in through the glass front door, you can see the store is trashed: stock that had been on the shelves appears to have been thrown about the store in a state of disarray.

Mattingly reports that at about 7:45 am, a black female whom he had never seen before, entered Bob's Market and placed several candy bars (totaling $11) in her pockets in an attempt to conceal them. Mattingly confronted the suspect but she refused to return the items and attempted to exit the business. Then, Mattingly locked the front door of the business using an electronic lock button located behind the counter. The suspect was not able to leave the business. The suspect then began damaging the consumable goods inside the store. After several minutes, Mattingly unlocked the door and the suspect fled the scene on foot.

Mattingly shows you the store's security video footage of the incident, stating that he can email you a copy of the video for evidence.

video: https://www.youtube.com/watch?v=ui0kYW82h4w&t=43s

Mattingly notes that the date on the video is incorrect: it should be 3-3-2018. The time is correct.

Field notes must be taken to gather the following information (at a minimum):

- Date/time of dispatch
- Full information on complainant
- Full information on victim (if different than the complainant)
- Full information on witnesses, if any
- Statement of nonconsent
- Description of damage
- Estimate of value of the damage and insurance information
- Description of suspect(s), if any

- Action taken (e.g., photos taken, description broadcast, area checked for suspects, summary of incident entered on roll call board)
- Notes should also include arrival time.

Suspect description protocol:
- Race/sex
- Approximate age
- Approximate height
- Approximate weight
- Hair length, style, and color
- Eye color (glasses worn—type)
- Clothing description (describe from head to toe)
- Name, or partial name, if known
- Scars, marks, tattoos
- Other characteristics (limp, stutter, braces on teeth, etc.)
- Associated vehicle

INCIDENT REPORT

Date:_____   Incident #_____

Nature of Incident:_____

Complainant:_____

Suspect:_____

Victim:_____

Witness #1:_____

Witness #2:_____

Witness #3:_____

Narrative:

_____

_____

_____

_____

_____

_____

_____

_____

_____

_____

_____

_____

_____

_____

_____

_____

_____

_____

_____

EXERCISE 5: Criminal Damage to Property

_____

● _____
_____
_____
_____
_____
_____
_____
_____
_____
_____
_____
_____
_____

● _____
_____
_____
_____
_____
_____
_____
_____
_____
_____
_____
_____
_____

Officer Signature _____

Officer Printed Name _____ Badge Number _____

EXERCISE 5: Criminal Damage to Property

RUBRIC

Requirement	Learner		Instructor	
	Included	Not Included	Included	Not Included
Student has reviewed the assignment scenario and video.				
Associated Competency **CO 2:** Differentiate reports based on type and purpose.				
Squad and shift assignment have been recorded in student's field notes.				
Time of dispatch and nature of assignment have been recorded in student's field notes.				
Observations of the scene (upon arrival and throughout investigation) have been recorded in student's field notes.				
Student has documented his or her performance of a medical assessment and rendering of first aid to the victim in his or her field notes.				
Names of complainant, victim, witnesses and suspect/arrestee have been recorded in student's field notes.				
Student has recorded a victim statement of nonconsent in his or her field notes.				
Student has recorded a description of damage to include an estimated $ amount of the damage and the name of the victim's insurance company in his or her field notes.				

A detailed description of the suspect is included in the student's field notes. Suspect description followed protocol.				
Any injuries to victims have been recorded in student notes.				
If photos of the scene were taken, student has documented, in his or her field notes, the subject of the photos and the number of photos taken.				
A photocopy of the student's field notes has been included with this assignment submission.				
Associated Competency **CO 3:** Demonstrate thorough preparation to develop a report.				
Student has documented his or her response to this assignment from beginning to end.				
Squad and shift assignment have been recorded in student's report narrative.				
Time of dispatch and nature of assignment have been recorded in student's report narrative.				
Observations of the scene (upon arrival and throughout investigation) have been recorded in student's report narrative.				
Narrative contains detailed, chronological descriptions of officer actions and observations.				
Names of complainant, victim, witnesses and suspect/arrestee have been recorded in student's report narrative along with any respective statements.				
Student has recorded a victim statement of nonconsent in his or her report narrative.				

Student has recorded a description of damage to include an estimated $ amount of the damage and the name of the victim's insurance company in his or her report narrative.				
Narrative documents a detailed description of the suspect, the investigative work done on the case, and the status of the investigation.				
If photos of the scene were taken, student has documented, in his or her report narrative, the subject of the photos and the number of photos taken.				
Report contains an "<u>Introduction</u>" paragraph as well as an "<u>Investigation</u>" paragraph and a "<u>Disposition</u>" paragraph.				
Associated Competency **CO 4:** Construct a narrative report in a chronological format.				
Submission is formatted as follows: 1. Student-completed rubric 2. Narrative report with student name, date, type of report, and incident # typed in a block in the upper right corner of page 1 of the report 3. Photocopy of student field notes				
The report is clear, legible, and free of errors or stray marks.				
The report evidences correct grammar, punctuation, spelling, and sentence structure.				
Associated Competency **CO 7:** Edit reports for compliance with associated rules of grammar and syntax.				
Learner has ensured that all elements of the rubric have been fulfilled and the deadline for this report has been met.				

EXERCISE 6

MUNICIPAL CITATION—DISORDERLY CONDUCT

Instructions: Using the information from this exercise, as well as your notes and report from Exercise 5, complete the municipal citation on the next page.

You have just received information regarding an arrest made in the Damage to Property complaint (Incident # 18-48751-332). On March 4, 2018, Detective Squad 115 (Swenson and Marcus), while investigating a similar incident at the Quicky Mart (8711 E. Franklin St. Appleton, WI 54911), arrested the suspect (listed below). The suspect also admitted vandalizing Bob's Market. Since you were the investigating officer on the Damage to Property at Bob's Market, you will issue a municipal citation for "Disorderly Conduct" to the suspect, in addition to the Criminal Damage to Property charges that will be requested based on your report from Exercise 5.

Suspect: Janice H. Foster, Female / Black, DOB 04-08-59, 7419 Wellington Way, Appleton, WI 54911, Ph. (920)487-6523, Employer: Guardian Defense Systems, Physical description: 5'8", 165 lbs, Brown Hair, Brown Eyes

Ordinance #17-6 (Damage to Property)

Venue: City of Appleton, Outagamie County, WI

Court date: April 19, 2018 at 8:30 am

Court Information:
Outagamie County Court Commissioner
320 Walnut Street
Appleton, WI 54911

Appearance in court is mandatory

Bond/forfeiture amount: $250.00

WISCONSIN UNIFORM MUNICIPAL COURT CITATION AND COMPLAINT

☐ Juvenile

*Deposit Permitted $_____

☐ Cash
☐ Card

(For Court Use only)

You Are Notified To Appear

Is this a mandatory appearance? ☐ yes ☐ no
(Read the reverse side of this citation for court information.)

Date _____

Time _____ ☐ AM ☐ PM

_____ Municipal Court

_____

Defendant Name - Last | First | MI

Street Address | Post Office | State | Zip Code

Driver License Number or Other I.D. (specify) | State | Exp. Yr.

Date of Birth | Sex | Race | Height | Weight | Hair | Eyes

License Plate Number | Plate Type | State | Exp. Yr.

Plaintiff: ☐ City ☐ Village ☐ Town
OF:

Defendant Violated:
Ordinance No.

Adopting State Statute No.

Description of Violation

Week Day | Month - Day - Year | Time | ☐ AM At: | ☐ PM County:

Name & Address of Parent/Guardian/Legal Custodian (if minor defendant)

Citation Served: ☐ Personally ☐ Mailed to defendant's last known address
☐ Left with person residing at defendant's residence: Name _____ Age _____

Print Officer Name | Department | I.D. No. | Date Citation Issued | Telephone Number of Parent/Guardian/Legal Custodian

MC-2000, 10/01

COURT COPY

AGENCY RECORD

Date of Disposition

PLEA: ☐ Guilty ☐ No Contest ☐ Not Guilty

Other Disposition:

FINDING: ☐ Guilty ☐ Default ☐ Not Guilty

☐ Dismissed ☐ Forfeiture $

Court Officer

Incident Report

Comments

POLICE REPORT WRITING
Exercise 6
Municipal Citation - Disorderly Conduct

RUBRIC

Requirement	Learner		Instructor	
	Included	Not Included	Included	Not Included
Student has reviewed the assignment scenario.				
Associated Competency **CO 2:** Differentiate reports based on type and purpose.				
Squad and shift assignment have been recorded in student's field notes.				
Time of dispatch and nature of assignment have been recorded in student's field notes.				
Observations of the scene (upon arrival and throughout investigation) have been recorded in student's field notes.				
Student has documented his or her performance of a medical assessment and rendering of first aid to the victim in his or her field notes.				
Any injuries to victims have been recorded in student notes.				
Names of complainant, victim, witnesses, and suspect/arrestee have been recorded in student's field notes.				
Student has recorded a victim statement of nonconsent in his or her field notes.				
A detailed description of the suspect is included in the student's field notes. Suspect description followed protocol.				
If photos of the scene were taken, student has documented, in his or her field notes, the subject of the photos and the number of photos taken.				

Associated Competency **CO 3:** Demonstrate thorough preparation to develop a report.				
All of the appropriate fields on the face of the municipal citation have been properly completed.				
Narrative documents the elements of Disorderly Conduct				
Narrative documents statements of complainants, victims, witnesses, and suspects.				
Narrative documents a detailed description of the suspect.				
If photos of the scene were taken, student has documented, in his or her citation narrative, the subject of the photos and the number of photos taken.				
A photocopy of the student's field notes has been included with this assignment submission.				
Associated Competency **CO 4:** Construct a narrative report in a chronological format.				
Submission is formatted as follows: 1. Student-completed rubric 2. Completed municipal citation (both front and back [narrative]) 3. Photocopy of student field notes				
The report is clear, legible, and free of errors or stray marks.				
The report evidences correct grammar, punctuation, spelling, and sentence structure.				
Associated Competency **CO 7:** Edit reports for compliance with associated rules of grammar and syntax.				
Learner has ensured that all elements of the rubric have been fulfilled and the deadline for this report has been met.				

EXERCISE 7

MUNICIPAL CITATION—THEFT

Relative to Criminal Damage to Property complaint from Exercise 5 (Incident # 18-48751-332), in addition to Foster being cited for Battery and charged with Criminal Damage to Property, you also issue her a municipal citation for shoplifting candy bars, in addition to the Criminal Damage to Property charges that will be requested based on your report from Exercise 5 and the Disorderly Conduct citation from Exercise 6.

Suspect: Janice H. Foster, Female / Black, DOB 04-08-59, 7419 Wellington Way, Appleton, WI 54911, Ph. (920)487-6523, Employer: Guardian Defense Systems, Physical description: 5'8", 165lbs, Brown Hair, Brown Eyes

Ordinance #32-3 (Shoplifting)

Venue: City of Appleton, Outagamie County, WI

Court date: April 19, 2018 at 8:30 am

Court Information:
Outagamie County Court Commissioner
320 Walnut Street
Appleton, WI 54911

Appearance in court is mandatory

Bond/forfeiture amount: $250.00

Instructions: Using the information from this exercise, as well as your notes and report from Exercise 5, complete the municipal citation on the next page.

WISCONSIN UNIFORM MUNICIPAL COURT CITATION AND COMPLAINT

☐ Juvenile

*Deposit Permitted
$ _____ ☐ Cash ☐ Card

(For Court Use only)

You Are Notified To Appear

Is this a mandatory appearance? ☐ yes ☐ no

(Read the reverse side of this citation for court information.)

Date _____

Time _____ ☐ AM ☐ PM

_____ Municipal Court

Defendant Name - Last		First		MI
Street Address		Post Office	State	Zip Code
Driver License Number or Other I.D. (specify)			State	Exp. Yr.

Date of Birth	Sex	Race	Height	Weight	Hair	Eyes

License Plate Number	Plate Type	State	Exp. Yr.

Plaintiff: ☐ City ☐ Village ☐ Town
OF:

Defendant Violated:

Ordinance No.

Adopting State Statute No.

Description of Violation

Week Day	Month - Day - Year	Time	☐ AM At:	Name & Address of Parent/Guardian/Legal Custodian (if minor defendant)
			☐ PM County:	

Citation Served: ☐ Personally ☐ Mailed to defendant's last known address

☐ Left with person residing at defendant's residence: Name _____ Age _____

Print Officer Name	Department	I.D. No.	Date Citation Issued	Telephone Number of Parent/Guardian/Legal Custodian

MC-2000, 10/01

COURT COPY

AGENCY RECORD

Date of Disposition

PLEA: ☐ Guilty ☐ No Contest ☐ Not Guilty

Other Disposition:

FINDING: ☐ Guilty ☐ Default ☐ Not Guilty ☐ Dismissed ☐ Forfeiture $ _____

Court Officer

Incident Report

Comments

POLICE REPORT WRITING
Exercise 7
Municipal Citation—Theft

RUBRIC

Requirement	Learner		Instructor	
	Included	Not Included	Included	Not Included
Student has reviewed the assignment scenario.				
Associated Competency **CO 2:** Differentiate reports based on type and purpose.				
Squad and shift assignment have been recorded in student's field notes.				
Time of dispatch and nature of assignment have been recorded in student's field notes.				
Observations of the scene (upon arrival and throughout investigation) have been recorded in student's field notes.				
A detailed description as well as a dollar value for the item taken has been documented in the student's field notes.				
Names of complainant, victim, witnesses, and suspect/arrestee have been recorded in student's field notes.				
Student has recorded a victim statement of nonconsent in his or her field notes.				
A detailed description of the suspect is included in the student's field notes. Suspect description followed protocol.				
A photocopy of the student's field notes has been included with this assignment submission.				
Associated Competency **CO 3:** Demonstrate thorough preparation to develop a report.				

All of the appropriate fields on the face of the municipal citation have been properly completed.				
Narrative documents the elements of Theft to include nonconsent.				
Narrative documents statements of complainants, victims, witnesses, and suspects.				
A detailed description as well as a dollar value for the item taken has been documented in the citation narrative.				
Narrative documents a detailed description of the suspect and/or how the suspect was identified.				
Student has recorded a victim statement of nonconsent in his or her citation narrative.				
Associated Competency **CO 4:** Construct a narrative report in a chronological format.				
Submission is formatted as follows: 1. Student-completed rubric 2. Completed municipal citation (both front and back [narrative]) 3. Photocopy of student field notes				
The report is clear, legible, and free of errors or stray marks.				
The report evidences correct grammar, punctuation, spelling, and sentence structure.				
Associated Competency **CO 7:** Edit reports for compliance with associated rules of grammar and syntax.				
Learner has ensured that all elements of the rubric have been fulfilled and the deadline for this report has been met.				

EXERCISE 8

DOMESTIC ABUSE NARRATIVE

Instructions: Use the information-gathering guide (below) to take notes as you view the video entitled, "Domestic in Progress." After viewing the video, complete a domestic abuse narrative based on the information that you have gathered, documenting your observations, the information that you gathered, and the resulting action that was taken.

Video: https://www.youtube.com/watch?v=cYycOSQOWTk

Information-gathering Guide:

- Domestic relationship?
- Has a crime been committed? Elements of crime(s)
- Full information on victim (including height/weight)
- Full information on suspect (including height/weight)
- Full information on witnesses, if any
- Statements by victim, suspect, witnesses
- Statement of nonconsent
- Victim's and suspect's demeanor and appearance
- Description of damage to property
- Description of injuries
- Evidence collected? Evidence identified and secured?
- Photos taken?
- Medical treatment? Release of medical information signed?
- Action taken (e.g., arrest, description of suspect if at large)

Incident # 18-000854-2217

Date/time of call: 6-12-2018 at 12:15 pm

Victim: Sarah T. Campbell, White / Female, DOB 1-17-81, 378 Florence Street Hermitage, PA 16159, Ph. 724-981-6193

Suspect: Bill V. Campbell, White / Male, DOB 7-23-1979, 378 Florence Street Hermitage, PA 16159, Ph. 724-981-6193

INCIDENT REPORT

Date:_____   Incident #_____

Nature of Incident:_____

Complainant:_____

Suspect:_____

Victim:_____

Witness #1:_____

Witness #2:_____

Witness #3:_____

Narrative:

_____

_____

_____

_____

_____

_____

_____

_____

_____

_____

_____

_____

_____

_____

_____

_____

_____

_____

_____

_____

_____

_____

_____

_____

_____

_____

_____

_____

_____

_____

_____

_____

_____

_____

_____

_____

_____

_____

_____

_____

_____

_____

_____

_____

_____

Officer Signature _____

Officer Printed Name _____ Badge Number _____

POLICE REPORT WRITING
Exercise 8
Domestic Abuse Narrative

RUBRIC

Requirement	Learner		Instructor	
	Included	Not Included	Included	Not Included
Student has reviewed the assignment scenario from the associated video.				
Associated Competency **CO 2:** Differentiate reports based on type and purpose.				
Squad and shift assignment have been recorded in student's field notes.				
Time of dispatch and nature of assignment have been recorded in student's field notes.				
Observations of the scene (upon arrival and throughout investigation) have been recorded in student's field notes.				
Student has documented his or her performance of a medical assessment and rendering of first aid to the victim in his or her field notes.				
Any injuries to victims have been recorded in student notes.				
Ambulance company name, squad #, and last names of personnel have been recorded in student's field notes.				

Names of complainant, victim, witnesses, and suspect/arrestee have been recorded in student's field notes.				
Student has recorded a victim statement of nonconsent in his or her field notes.				
Associated Competency **CO 3:** Demonstrate thorough preparation to develop a report.				
Squad and shift assignment have been recorded in student's narrative report.				
Time of dispatch and nature of assignment have been recorded in student's narrative report.				
Observations of the scene (upon arrival and throughout investigation) have been recorded in student's narrative report.				
Student has documented nature of relationship between the suspect and victim(s). · Live(d) together · Married · Have children in common				
Student has documented evidence collected to include precise record of chain of custody and date, time, and location of inventory, as well as inventory number.				
If victim required medical attention at a hospital, student has recorded the ambulance company name, squad #, and last names of personnel transporting the victim as well as the hospital to which the victim was transported.				
If photos of the scene were taken, student has documented, in his or her field notes, the subject of the photos and the number of photos taken.				

A photocopy of the student's field notes has been included with this assignment submission.				
Narrative documents the elements of the domestic offense to include nonconsent.				
Narrative documents statements of complainants, victims, witnesses, and suspects.				
Narrative documents a detailed explanation of work performed on the case and any areas requiring follow-up description of the suspect.				
Associated Competency **CO 4:** Construct a narrative report in a chronological format.				
Submission is formatted as follows: 1. Student-completed rubric 2. Narrative report 3. Photocopy of student field notes				
The report is clear, legible, and free of errors or stray marks.				
The report evidences correct grammar, punctuation, spelling, and sentence structure.				
Associated Competency **CO 7:** Edit reports for compliance with associated rules of grammar and syntax.				
Learner has ensured that all elements of the rubric have been fulfilled and the deadline for this report has been met.				

EMERGENCY DETENTION—MENTAL HEALTH

Instructions: After taking field notes while reading the scenario and watching the video, complete an emergency detention report.

Scenario: On 08/29/2018 at 3:45 pm you are called to the intersection of N. Boca Vista Blvd. and Main Street, City of Green Bay, about a disorderly individual. The complainant indicated to dispatch that the subject, a white male with no shirt on, was running around in the street, harassing traffic, punching car windows. The subject also picked up a bike and threw it into a car windshield.

Upon arrival you find a white male with his shirt off lying on the street, bleeding from his right side. Standing by him is a white male trying to calm him down. There is a car stopped about 10 feet in front of the bleeding subject, standing with both front doors open. The bleeding subject is attempting to get up, but repeatedly falls back down. You attempt to calm the individual, telling him to stay on the ground. You also call dispatch and request an ambulance for him. With help from another responding officer, Officer Samuel Vega (Squad #153), you are able to gain compliance from the individual, who simply remains laying on his back moaning until the ambulance arrives. While waiting for the ambulance, you search the subject. You find a wallet containing a Wisconsin Driver License with the bleeding subject's picture on it, identifying him as Ernest Olson. The ambulance crew assesses his injuries, secures him to a gurney, and transports him to the hospital. Officer Vega follows the ambulance to the hospital.

After the ambulance leaves, you speak with the subject who was attempting to calm Olson when you arrived. You identify this subject as Robert Shain. Shain tells you that he had been driving north on Boca Vista Blvd. when he saw Olson walking in the roadway. Olson walked up to Shain's car and Shain stopped. Olson said to Shain that he needed to go to the hospital, and asked if Shain would take him. Olson then got into Shain's car, without Shain saying whether he would take Olson to the hospital. Shain drove northbound on Boca Vista Blvd. up to the next intersection (Main Street). At that point, Olson screamed aloud, opened his door and lept from the car while it was still moving, causing the wound that you observed on Olson. Shain stopped his car and got out to see if Olson needed help. This was when you arrived on scene. Shain does not know Olson.

After interviewing Shain, you go to 2372 Boca Vista Blvd. to interview the complainant Rodney Piccard. Upon arrival, Piccard states that a white male with no shirt on was running around in the street, hassling people in traffic, punching car windows. The subject also picked up a bike and threw it into a car windshield. He then produces his girlfriend's smartphone and shows you the following video:

Video: https://www.youtube.com/watch?v=tozzTaF9IHc

Piccard's girlfriend, Amanda Jacobs, was watching the incident with him. She is at Piccard's apartment when you arrive. Piccard offers to email you the video.

After you complete your interview of Piccard and Jacobs, you drive to St. Vincent's Hospital and meet with Officer Vega. He informs you that Crisis Intervention Social Worker Newton and County Mental Health Caseworker Nyman concur that Olson should be held on a mental health hold. They have both had contact with him in the past, and inform you that he has severe schizophrenia, and he needs inpatient treatment. Upon his medical release, you transport Olson to Brown County Mental Health Facility and turn him over to Caseworker Nyman.

Protective Custody Conveyance (Mental Health Hold)

Field notes must be taken to gather the following information (at a minimum):

- Basis for contact with subject
- Full information on complainant, if available
- Full information on witnesses, if any
- Full information on subject
- Witness statements
- Observations of subject's condition/behavior
  - Evidence of alcohol/drug use?
  - Evidence of incapacitation?
  - Subject statements, demeanor
- Explicit statement of officer's conclusion that subject was incapacitated by alcohol
- Medical treatment?
- Time of medical release from emergency room and name of releasing authority
- Handcuffed?
- Transport and turnover to medical detoxification facility
- Date and time that turnover was completed
- Name of detoxification facility worker who accepted the subject

Further Information:

Incident # 18-00443-5630

Squad #: 187

Date/time of call: June 23, 2018 at 2 pm

Complainant: Rodney M. Piccard, White / Male, DOB: 02-14-80, 2372 Boca Vista Blvd., Green Bay, WI 54221, Ph. (920)447-2315

Witness: Amanda C. Jacobs, White / Female, DOB: 1-17-81, 2372 Boca Vista Blvd., Green Bay, WI 54221, Ph. (920)447-2315

Emotionally Disturbed Person: Ernest H. Olson, White / Male, DOB: 9-27-85, 3816 Hummingbird Lane, Green Bay, WI 54221, Ph. (920)385-7142

Witness: Robert L. Shain, White / Male, DOB 5-15-1961, 3197 Jewell Road, Green Bay, WI 54221, Ph. (920)621-1899

Ambulance: Blue Cross Ambulance (EMT C. Martin, Paramedics V. Williams and T. Julius)

Hospital: St. Vincent Hospital

Crisis Intervention Specialist: Connie S. Newton, Black / Female, DOB: 8-23-70, 4716 N. 14th St., Green Bay, WI 54307, Ph. (920)864-0036

Brown County Mental Health Facility Caseworker: Tommy B. Nyman, Black / Male, DOB: 07-23-67, 4632 Benevolent Way, Green Bay, WI 54307, Ph. (920)227-7673

INCIDENT REPORT

Date:_____   Incident #_____

Nature of Incident:_____

Complainant:_____

Suspect:_____

Victim:_____

Witness #1:_____

Witness #2:_____

Witness #3:_____

Narrative:

_____

_____

_____

_____

_____

_____

_____

_____

_____

_____

_____

_____

_____

_____

_____

_____

_____

_____

_____

_____

_____

_____

_____

_____

_____

_____

_____

_____

_____

_____

_____

_____

_____

_____

_____

_____

_____

_____

_____

_____

_____

_____

_____

Officer Signature _____

Officer Printed Name _____ Badge Number _____

POLICE REPORT WRITING
Exercise 9A
Emergency Detention Mental/Drug/Alcohol

RUBRIC

Requirement	Learner		Instructor	
	Included	Not Included	Included	Not Included
Student has reviewed the assignment scenario and the associated video segment.				
Associated Competency **CO 2:** Differentiate reports based on type and purpose.				
Squad and shift assignment have been recorded in student's field notes.				
Time of dispatch and nature of assignment have been recorded in student's field notes.				
Observations of the scene (upon arrival and throughout investigation) have been recorded in student's field notes.				
Student has documented his or her performance of a medical assessment and any rendering of needed first aid to the victim in his or her field notes.				
Any injuries to victims have been recorded in the student's field notes.				
Ambulance company name, squad #, and last names of personnel have been recorded in student's field notes.				

Names of complainant, victim, witnesses, and suspect/arrestee have been recorded in student's field notes.				
Student has recorded a victim statement in his or her field notes.				
Student has noted own personal observations in his or her field notes.				
Associated Competency **CO 3:** Demonstrate thorough preparation to develop a report.				
Time of dispatch and nature of assignment have been recorded in student's report narrative.				
Squad and shift assignment have been recorded in student's report narrative.				
Observations of the scene (upon arrival and throughout investigation) have been recorded in student's report narrative.				
Student has documented his or her performance of a medical assessment and any rendering of needed first aid to the victim in his or her report narrative.				
Any injuries to victims have been recorded in the student's report narrative.				
Ambulance company name, squad #, and last names of personnel have been recorded in student's narrative report.				
Narrative documents statements of complainants, victims, witnesses, and suspects.				

Student has documented the notification of Crisis Intervention and the name of the person that arranged a place for the detention in the report narrative.				
Student has documented that the victim has been medically cleared by hospital personnel and who the clearing authority is.				
Student has documented the time of transport to either Brown County Mental Health Facility or New Beginnings Detox Center as well as who the victim was turned over to.				
Associated Competency **CO 4:** Construct a narrative report in a chronological format.				
Submission is formatted as follows: 1. Student-completed rubric 2. Narrative report 3. Photocopy of student field notes				
The report is formatted as follows: · 1-inch margin · Double-spaced text · 12-point font				
The report is clear, legible, and free of errors or stray marks.				
The report evidences correct grammar, punctuation, spelling, and sentence structure.				
Associated Competency **CO 7:** Edit reports for compliance with associated rules of grammar and syntax.				
Learner has ensured that all elements of the rubric have been fulfilled and the deadline for this report has been met.				

EXERCISE 9B

EMERGENCY DETENTION—ALCOHOL INCAPACITATION

Instructions: After taking field notes while reading the scenario and watching the video, complete an emergency detention report.

Scenario: On 08/29/2018 at 3:45 pm, you are called to Quicky Mart at 2834 Trails End Road, Howard, WI 54303 about a drunken individual. When you arrive, you find a subject, Charles Norton, lying on his back on the sidewalk outside of the Quicky Mart, in and out of consciousness. You notify dispatch and request that an ambulance respond to the scene. While waiting for the ambulance, you speak with the clerk, James Kilby. He tells you that the subject entered the store, apparently to buy beer. He was unable to maintain his balance, falling often, requiring support to walk, and knocking items off the shelves. Kilby called for police because he was concerned for the subject's safety.

After the ambulance arrives and you turn Norton over to the ambulance crew, Kilby informs you that there is store surveillance video of the incident, which he plays for you.

Video: https://www.youtube.com/watch?v=Ti3UL_mVHHI&t=155s

The ambulance transported Norton to Mercy Medical Center. You go to Mercy after you complete your interview of Kilby. While Norton is being checked by physicians, you contact the County Crisis Intervention Specialist who then arranges a bed for Norton at the New Beginnings Detoxification Center. Upon his medical release, you transport Norton to Detox and turn him over to the on-duty counselor.

Further information:

Incident # 18-00485-9932

Squad #: 187

Caller: James C. Kilby (store clerk): White / Male, DOB: 3-16-59, 2229 Country Lane Ashwaubenon, WI 54332, Ph. (920)965-2112

Drunken Person: Charles M. Norton, White / Male, DOB: 6-02-88, 623 S. 45th St., De Pere, WI 54321, Ph. (920)845-4230

Ambulance: Blue Cross Ambulance (EMT A. Robertson and Paramedics B. Mantle and R. Jorgenson)

Hospital: Mercy Medical Center

Crisis Intervention Social Worker: Douglas H. Colby, White / Male, DOB: 4-14-78, 7165 W. Dickenson Dr., Green Bay, WI 54307, Ph. (920)483-1010

New Beginnings Detoxification Center Caseworker: Rodney A. Talbert White / Male, DOB: 01-07-83, 325 E. Oakdale Dr., Green Bay, WI 54307, Ph. (920)273-4419

Field notes must be taken to gather the following information (at a minimum):

- Basis for contact with subject
- Full information on complainant, if available
- Full information on witnesses, if any
- Full information on subject
- Witness statements
- Observations of subject's condition/behavior
    - Evidence of alcohol use
    - Evidence of incapacitation
    - Subject statements, demeanor
- Explicit statement of officer's conclusion that subject was incapacitated by alcohol
- Medical treatment?
- Time of medical release from emergency room and name of releasing authority
- Handcuffed?
- Transport and turnover to medical detoxification facility
- Date and time that turnover was completed
- Name of detoxification facility worker who accepted the subject

INCIDENT REPORT

Date:_____   Incident #_____

Nature of Incident:_____

Complainant:_____

Suspect:_____

Victim:_____

Witness #1:_____

Witness #2:_____

Witness #3:_____

Narrative:

_____

_____

_____

_____

_____

_____

_____

_____

_____

_____

_____

_____

_____

_____

_____

_____

_____

_____

_____

EXERCISE 9B: Emergency Detention—Alcohol Incapacitation

Officer Signature _____

Officer Printed Name _____ Badge Number _____

EXERCISE 9B: Emergency Detention—Alcohol Incapacitation

POLICE REPORT WRITING
Exercise 9B
Emergency Detention Mental/Drug/Alcohol

RUBRIC

	Learner		Instructor	
Requirement	Included	Not Included	Included	Not Included
Student has reviewed the assignment scenario and video segment.				
Associated Competency **CO 2:** Differentiate reports based on type and purpose.				
Squad and shift assignment have been recorded in student's field notes.				
Time of dispatch and nature of assignment have been recorded in student's field notes.				
Observations of the scene (upon arrival and throughout investigation) have been recorded in student's field notes.				
Student has documented his or her performance of a medical assessment and any rendering of needed first aid to the victim in his or her field notes.				
Any injuries to victims have been recorded in student notes.				
Ambulance company name, squad #, and last names of personnel have been recorded in student's field notes.				
Names of complainant, victim, witnesses, and suspect/arrestee have been recorded in student's field notes.				

Student has recorded a victim statement in his or her field notes.				
Student has noted own personal observations in his or her field notes.				
Associated Competency **CO 3:** Demonstrate thorough preparation to develop a report.				
Time of dispatch and nature of assignment have been recorded in student's report narrative.				
Squad and shift assignment have been recorded in student's report narrative.				
Observations of the scene (upon arrival and throughout investigation) have been recorded in student's report narrative.				
Student has documented his or her performance of a medical assessment and any rendering of needed first aid to the victim in his or her report narrative.				
Any injuries to victims have been recorded in student report narrative.				
Ambulance company name, squad #, and last names of personnel have been recorded in student's narrative report.				
Narrative documents statements of complainants, victims, witnesses, and suspects.				
Student has documented the notification of Crisis Intervention and the name of the person who arranged a place for the detention.				

Student has documented that the victim has been medically cleared by hospital personnel and who the clearing authority is.				
Student has documented the time of transport to either Brown County Mental Health Facility or New Beginnings Detox Center as well as who the victim was turned over to.				
Associated Competency **CO 4:** Construct a narrative report in a chronological format.				
Submission is formatted as follows: 1. Student-completed rubric 2. Narrative report 3. Photocopy of student field notes				
The report is formatted as follows: · 1-inch margin · Double-spaced text · 12-point font				
The report is clear, legible, and free of errors or stray marks.				
The report evidences correct grammar, punctuation, spelling, and sentence structure.				
Associated Competency **CO 7:** Edit reports for compliance with associated rules of grammar and syntax.				
Learner has ensured that all elements of the rubric have been fulfilled and the deadline for this report has been met.				

EXERCISE 10

DISORDERLY CONDUCT

Instructions: After taking field notes while reading the scenario and viewing the video, compose a disorderly conduct report (Incident # 18-48714-312).

On July 6, 2018, at 12:47 pm, you are called to respond to The Burgermeister Restaurant in the Cedar Valley Mall, 3916 S. Edgar Lane, Green Bay, WI for Disorderly Customers complaint. Upon arrival, you are met by the manager, Robert B. Jensen, White / Male, DOB 11-02-59, of 2345 N. Sycamore Dr., Green Bay, WI 54307, Ph. (920)688-1133, who is also the complainant in this incident. Jensen states that at about 12:30 pm a white male (Suspect) came by the restaurant and attempted to order food. He was obviously intoxicated, smelling of liquor and slurring his speech. Jensen the clerk was unable to understand what the suspect was trying to say when he ordered his food. The suspect began to berate the clerk verbally, calling her stupid. One of the customers, a black male wearing a stocking cap standing by the soft drink machine, told the suspect to leave because the suspect was drunk. At this point the suspect walked over by that customer, and slapped the customer in the face after a short verbal altercation. Jensen stopped watching at this point and ran to call the police.

Jensen states that he was uninjured by the suspect, nor was any damage done to restaurant. He does not know what happened to the suspect, as the suspect and all of the customers but one had left the restaurant by the time he returned from calling the police. Jensen would like something done because the entire incident startled his customers and disrupted their experience. As a result of this incident, approximately six of his customers left his restaurant without ordering food.

The customer that stayed after the fight, Carrie J. Silvers, White / Female, DOB. 05-07-1990 of 1090 Spadafore Drive, Green Bay, WI 54307, Ph. 920-808-6672, stated that she was eating her lunch at the time of the incident. After the suspect started to verbally abuse the clerk, Silvers activated the video recorded on her phone. She showed you the video and offered to email it to you. Silvers stated that she saw the suspect leave through the door next to her table (westbound) into the mall, while the customer that the suspect struck left the restaurant through the main entrance (northbound) into the mall. The customers all left through the main entrance as well.

Video: https://www.youtube.com/watch?v=A00weMt9Gl4

Field notes must be taken to gather the following information (at a minimum):

- Date/time of dispatch
- Full information on complainant
- Full information on victim (if different than the complainant)
- Full information on witnesses, if any
- Description of disturbance
- Description of suspect(s), if any
- Description of witnesses
- Action taken (e.g., photos taken, description broadcast, area checked for suspects, summary of incident entered on roll call board)
- Notes should also include arrival time.

Suspect description protocol:

- Race/sex
- Approximate age
- Approximate height
- Approximate weight
- Hair length, style, and color
- Eye color (glasses worn—type)
- Clothing description (describe from head to toe)
- Name, or partial name, if known
- Scars, marks, tattoos
- Other characteristics (limp, stutter, braces on teeth, etc.)
- Associated vehicle

For this report, you should also generate descriptions of the suspect, the customer he struck, as well as the witnesses that left the scene based on your video observations.

INCIDENT REPORT

Date:_____   Incident #_____

Nature of Incident:_____

Complainant:_____

Suspect:_____

Victim:_____

Witness #1:_____

Witness #2:_____

Witness #3:_____

Narrative:

_____

_____

_____

_____

_____

_____

_____

_____

_____

_____

_____

_____

_____

_____

_____

_____

_____

_____

EXERCISE 10: Disorderly Conduct

_____

_____

_____

_____

_____

_____

_____

_____

_____

_____

_____

_____

_____

_____

_____

_____

_____

_____

_____

_____

_____

_____

_____

Officer Signature _____

Officer Printed Name _____ Badge Number _____

POLICE REPORT WRITING
Exercise 10
Disorderly Conduct Narrative

RUBRIC

Requirement	Learner		Instructor	
	Included	Not Included	Included	Not Included
Student has reviewed the assignment scenario and the associated video segment.				
Associated Competency **CO 2:** Differentiate reports based on type and purpose.				
Squad and shift assignment have been recorded in student's field notes.				
Time of dispatch and nature of assignment have been recorded in student's field notes.				
Observations of the scene (upon arrival and throughout investigation) have been recorded in student's field notes.				
Names of complainant, victim, witnesses, and suspect/arrestee (if known) have been recorded in student's field notes.				
A detailed description of the suspect(s) is included in the student's field notes. Suspect description followed protocol.				
A photocopy of the student's field notes has been included with this assignment submission.				

Associated Competency **CO 3:** Demonstrate thorough preparation to develop a report.				
Student has documented his or her response to this assignment from beginning to end.				
Squad and shift assignment have been recorded in student's report narrative.				
Time of dispatch and nature of assignment have been recorded in student's report narrative.				
Observations of the scene (upon arrival and throughout investigation) have been recorded in student's report narrative.				
Names of complainant, victim, witnesses, and suspect/arrestee have been recorded in student's report narrative.				
Facts meeting the elements of a crime charged have been articulated in the student's report narrative.				
Venue in which incident occurred has been articulated in student's report narrative.				
Report contains an "Introduction" paragraph as well as an "Investigation" paragraph and a "Disposition" paragraph.				
Associated Competency **CO 4:** Construct a narrative report in a chronological format.				

Submission is formatted as follows: 1. Student-completed rubric 2. Narrative report with student name, date, type of report, and incident # typed in a block in the upper right corner of page 1 of the report 3. Photocopy of student field notes			
The report is clear, legible, and free of errors or stray marks.			
The report evidences correct grammar, punctuation, spelling, and sentence structure.			
Associated Competency **CO 7:** Edit reports for compliance with associated rules of grammar and syntax.			
Learner has ensured that all elements of the rubric have been fulfilled and the deadline for this report has been met.			

MISSING PERSON—ENDANGERED NARRATIVE REPORT

Instructions: After reviewing the associated missing person poster and the reporting party information and statement, you will use the information that you have gathered to complete a missing person report narrative (Incident # 18-513-477).

MISSING PERSON—ENDANGERED

ANDREW RICHARDSON
Missing: November 6, 2018
DOB: 4/9/2010
Age Now: 8
Sex: Male
Race: Black
Hair: Lt. Brown
Eye Color: Hazel
Height: 3'10"
Weight: 60 lbs
Missing From: Milwaukee, Wisconsin

MARIANA FARAH SALDIVAR
Abductor
DOB: 11/25/1977
Sex: Female
Race: Hispanic
Hair: Brown
Eyes: Brown
Height: 5'6"
Weight: 130 lbs

On November 6, 2018, you are called to respond to the report of a missing child at 8319 N. Windmere Ct., in the City and County of Milwaukee. Upon arrival, you meet the complainant/reporting person, Antonio P. Richardson, Black / Male, DOB: 3-27-81, of 8319 N. Windmere Ct., Milwaukee, WI 53208, Ph. (414)257-4314. Richardson states that he and his girlfriend, Mariana Farah Saldivar, Hispanic / Female, 11-25-77 of 8319 N. Windmere Ct., Milwaukee, WI 53208, Ph. (414)257-4314, recently had an argument over how to best provide for their son, Andrew C. Richardson, Black / Male, DOB: 04-09-2012. Antonio said that the argument had taken place at their residence on Monday, November 5, 2018, at approximately 10:00 pm. The argument occurred because Mariana did not believe that Antonio, as a construction worker, would be able to adequately provide for her and Andrew. At the time of the argument, Andrew was sleeping in his bedroom. Since they could not reach a resolution, Antonio slept in a guest bedroom and Mariana slept in the master bedroom. When Antonio awoke this morning at approximately 7 am, he discovered that both Andrew and Saldivar were gone. He assumed that she had left the house early to go to work and drop Andrew off at school on the way. At 3:30 pm today, Antonio received a call from Principal John Davis at Brentwood Elementary School. Principal Davis was calling to find out if Andrew was okay because he never arrived at school today. Immediately after the call from Principal Davis, Antonio called Mariana on her cell phone. She answered and told Antonio that she was fed up with her life with him and that she and Andrew were on their way to a new and better life without him (Antonio) in it. Mariana then hung up the phone. Antonio tried to call Mariana back, but received no answer. At approximately 4:00 pm he attempted to contact Mariana at her workplace (Acme Plastics), but was informed by the Foreman, Rick Sanchez, that Mariana had failed to show up for work today. To Antonio's knowledge, Saldivar has only two friends in the area: Jacqueline C. Post, White / Female, DOB 04-14-1982, of 4518 Wellington Dr., Racine WI 54707, Ph. (262)593-8523 (Post also works at Acme Plastics) and Albert V. Roddick, Black / Male, DOB: 10-01-1975, of 4300 W. 115th St., Wauwatosa, WI 53115, Ph. (414)776-2890. Albert is Mariana's Alcoholics Anonymous (AA) sponsor. Antonio had heard Mariana mention several times that if she ever left him, she would take Andrew to live with her mother, Esperanza Saldivar, in Tijuana, Mexico.

According to Antonio, Saldivar drives a 2008, Pontiac, G-6, 2 door, black, bearing Wisconsin Automobile Plates CHH-473. The vehicle has scrapes and a large dent to the right, front fender after recently being involved in an automobile accident.

Field notes must be taken to gather the following information (at a minimum):

- Your arrival time
- Name, DOB, and full description of juvenile (including any mental incapacitation, medical, drug or alcohol issues, and clothing when last seen)
- Full information on complainant (Parent? Guardian?)
- Status of juvenile (Child Protective Services petition? Capias issued?)
- Time frame of disappearance? Last seen/contacted?
- Places juvenile might be?
- Information (names, phone numbers, addresses) of friends
- Juvenile entered into NCIC? Description broadcast?
- Action taken (Search home? Other interviews? Canvas neighborhood? Disposition?)

Suspect description protocol:

- Race/sex
- Approximate age
- Approximate height
- Approximate weight
- Hair length, style, and color
- Eye color (glasses worn—type)
- Clothing description (describe from head to toe)
- Name, or partial name, if known
- Scars, marks, tattoos
- Other characteristics (limp, stutter, braces on teeth, etc.)
- Associated vehicle

Upon completion of your field notes, write a detailed Missing Person narrative report documenting what was reported and the details of your investigation.

INCIDENT REPORT

Date:_____   Incident #_____

Nature of Incident:_____

Complainant:_____

Suspect:_____

Victim:_____

Witness #1:_____

Witness #2:_____

Witness #3:_____

Narrative:

_____

_____

_____

_____

_____

_____

_____

_____

_____

_____

_____

_____

_____

_____

_____

_____

_____

_____

_____

_____

_____

_____

_____

_____

_____

_____

_____

_____

_____

_____

_____

_____

_____

_____

_____

_____

_____

_____

_____

_____

_____

Officer Signature _____

Officer Printed Name _____ Badge Number _____

POLICE REPORT WRITING
Exercise 11A
Missing Person/Runaway Narrative Report

RUBRIC

Requirement	Learner		Instructor	
	Included	Not Included	Included	Not Included
Student has reviewed the assignment scenario and related missing person poster.				
Associated Competency **CO 2:** Differentiate reports based on type and purpose.				
Squad and shift assignment have been recorded in student's field notes.				
Time of dispatch and nature of assignment have been recorded in student's field notes.				
Observations of the scene (upon arrival and throughout investigation) have been recorded in student's field notes.				
Names of complainant, victim, witnesses, and suspect/arrestee have been recorded in student's field notes.				
Student has recorded a victim statement of nonconsent in his or her field notes.				
A detailed description of the suspect(s) is included in the student's field notes. Suspect description followed protocol.				
A photocopy of the student's field notes has been included with this assignment submission.				

Associated Competency **CO 3:** Demonstrate thorough preparation to develop a report.			
Student has documented his or her response to this assignment from beginning to end.			
Squad and shift assignment have been recorded in student's report narrative.			
Time of dispatch and nature of assignment have been recorded in student's report narrative.			
Observations of the scene (upon arrival and throughout investigation) have been recorded in student's report narrative.			
Names of complainant, victim, witnesses, and suspect/arrestee have been recorded in student's report narrative.			
Student has recorded a victim/witness statement in his or her report narrative.			
Student has articulated facts that meet statutory elements in the report narrative.			
A detailed description of the suspect(s) is included in the student's report narrative. Suspect description followed protocol.			
Venue in which incident occurred has been articulated in student's report narrative.			
Submission is formatted as follows: 1. Student-completed rubric 2. Narrative report with student name, date, type of report, and incident # typed in a block in the upper right corner of page 1 of the report 3. Photocopy of student field notes			

The report is clear, legible, and free of errors or stray marks.				
The report evidences correct grammar, punctuation, spelling, and sentence structure.				
Associated Competency **CO 7:** Edit reports for compliance with associated rules of grammar and syntax.				
Learner has ensured that all elements of the rubric have been fulfilled and the deadline for this report has been met.				

EXERCISE 11B

MISSING PERSON/RUNAWAY NARRATIVE REPORT

Instructions: After reviewing the associated runaway child poster and the reporting party information and statement, you will use the information that you have gathered to complete a runaway report narrative (Incident # 18-513-483).

Missing Juvenile

Name: Gene J. Cloud

DOB: December 7, 2002

Missing: February 28, 2018

Age: 15

Sex: Male

Race: Native American

Hair Color: Black

Eye Color: Brown

Height: 5'8"

Weight: 140 lbs

Missing From: Black River Falls, Wisconsin

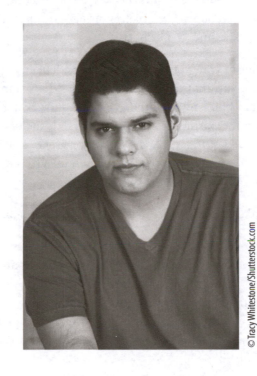

© Tracy Whitestone/Shutterstock.com

General information

On February 28, 2018, at 10:05 pm, you are called to respond to the report of a Runaway Teen at 1322 Rockaway Drive, in the Village of Black River Falls, Jackson County, WI. Upon arrival, you meet the complainant/reporting person, DeForest M. Cloud, Native American / Male, DOB: 07-21-1975 of 19 Eagleview Trail, Black River Falls, WI 51134, Ph. (715)574-3148. DeForest states that his son, Gene Cloud, has been a repeated runaway. This morning, at 7:30 am, before leaving for school, Gene approached DeForest and asked him if he could stay overnight at the home of his girlfriend, Amy M. Doxtator, Native American / Female, DOB: 03-29-2002, of 217 Wolverine Pass, Black River Falls, WI 51134, Ph. (715)886-0003. When Deforest forbid Gene to stay overnight at any girl's house, Gene became angry and shouted at DeForest that he would "stay any damn place he pleased," and he left abruptly, slamming the door behind him. Later this afternoon (approximately 3:45 pm), Deforest contacted Janice Teal, the Secretary at Central High School, to discover that Gene had not attended school today. Since Gene has not yet returned home, DeForest has contacted you, to file a runaway report. DeForest allows you to check his entire residence to ensure that Gene had not returned home without his knowledge. Amy Doxtator's parents are: Mother: Elsie B. Doxtator, Native American / Female, DOB: 05-13-73; Stepfather: Weaver D. Sims, Black / Male, DOB: 02-23-70, both share the same address and phone number as Amy. A classmate, Leslie R. Metoxen, Native American / Female, DOB: 01-28-96, 2214 Bengali Way, Black River Falls, WI 51134, Ph. 715-585-6172, was the last person to see Gene. She observed him as she was on the way to school on February 28, 2018, at approximately 9:00 am near the Millston area in southern Jackson County. Metoxen said she saw Gene walking on Highway O, but his whereabouts since that time are unknown. Gene was last seen wearing a black stocking hat, black jeans, a red hooded sweatshirt, a black leather jacket, and black shoes.

During your investigation, you go to the Doxtator residence at approximately 11:30 pm. Elsie and Weaver are cooperative, but tell you that they hadn't even heard anything about Gene running away, nor had they recently seen him. They call Amy into the living room to ask her if she has recently seen Gene. She denied seeing him at all within the past few days and claims that she doesn't know where he is. You obtain permission, from Elsie and Weaver, to search the house for Gene. During the search, you discover him hiding in the basement, behind some storage boxes. You then take him into custody at 11:45 pm, and return him to his father at 12:45 am on March 1.

Field notes must be taken to gather the following information (at a minimum):

- Your arrival time
- Name, DOB, and full description of juvenile (including any mental incapacitation, medical, drug or alcohol issues, and clothing when last seen)
- Full information on complainant (Parent? Guardian?)
- Status of juvenile (Child Protective Services petition? Capias issued?)
- History of behavior problems (e.g., prior running away)? Or is this a significant departure from normal?
- Possibility of foul play?
- Time frame of disappearance? Last seen/contacted?
- Places juvenile might be?
- Information (names, phone numbers, addresses) of friends
- Juvenile entered into NCIC? Description broadcast?
- Action taken (Search home? Other interviews? Canvas neighborhood? Disposition?)

-

INCIDENT REPORT

Date:_____   Incident #_____

Nature of Incident:_____

Complainant:_____

Suspect:_____

Victim:_____

Witness #1:_____

Witness #2:_____

Witness #3:_____

Narrative:

_____

_____

_____

_____

_____

_____

_____

_____

_____

_____

_____

_____

_____

_____

_____

_____

_____

_____

EXERCISE 11B: Missing Person/Runaway Narrative Report

_____

_____

_____

_____

_____

_____

_____

_____

_____

_____

_____

_____

_____

_____

_____

_____

_____

_____

_____

_____

_____

_____

_____

_____

_____

Officer Signature _____

Officer Printed Name _____ Badge Number _____

POLICE REPORT WRITING
Exercise 11B
Missing Person/Runaway Narrative Report

RUBRIC

Requirement	Learner		Instructor	
	Included	Not Included	Included	Not Included
Student has reviewed the assignment scenario and related runaway poster.				
Associated Competency CO 2: Differentiate reports based on type and purpose.				
Squad and shift assignment have been recorded in student's field notes.				
Time of dispatch and nature of assignment have been recorded in student's field notes.				
Observations of the scene (upon arrival and throughout investigation) have been recorded in student's field notes.				
Names of complainant, victim, witnesses, and suspect/arrestee have been recorded in student's field notes.				
A detailed description of the suspect(s) is included in the student's field notes. Suspect description followed protocol.				
A photocopy of the student's field notes has been included with this assignment submission.				
Associated Competency CO 3: Demonstrate thorough preparation to develop a report.				

Student has documented his or her response to this assignment from beginning to end.			
Squad and shift assignment have been recorded in student's report narrative.			
Time of dispatch and nature of assignment have been recorded in student's report narrative.			
Observations of the scene (upon arrival and throughout investigation) have been recorded in student's report narrative.			
Names of complainant, victim, witnesses, and suspect/arrestee have been recorded in student's report narrative.			
Student has recorded a victim/witness statement in his or her report narrative.			
Student has articulated facts that meet statutory elements in the report narrative.			
A detailed description of the suspect(s) is included in the student's report narrative. Suspect description followed protocol.			
Venue in which incident occurred has been articulated in student's report narrative.			
Submission is formatted as follows: 1. Student-completed rubric 2. Narrative report with student name, date, type of report, and incident # typed in a block in the upper right corner of page 1 of the report 3. Photocopy of student field notes			
The report is clear, legible, and free of errors or stray marks.			

EXERCISE 11B: Missing Person/Runaway Narrative Report

The report evidences correct grammar, punctuation, spelling, and sentence structure.				
Associated Competency **CO 7:** Edit reports for compliance with associated rules of grammar and syntax.				
Learner has ensured that all elements of the rubric have been fulfilled and the deadline for this report has been met.				

MOTOR VEHICLE THEFT

Instructions: Upon completion of your field notes, write a detailed offense report documenting what was reported and the details of your investigation.

On March 19, 2018, at 4:30 pm you are called to respond to 9137 Harbor Dr., Green Bay, WI for a stolen automobile complaint. Upon arrival, you are met by Cody R. Johnson, W/M, DOB: 09-14-94, 9137 Harbor Dr., Green Bay, WI 54917, Ph. (920)738-4142, who said that an unknown person stole his black 1995 Jeep Grand Cherokee 4-door, Wisconsin Automobile Plates EPX449. Upon arrival, you interview Cody, who states that he works third shift at Acme Plumbing Supply factory. When he got home this morning, he parked his Grand Cherokee across the road from his home. He locked the doors. He then went in his house and went to bed. When he woke up this afternoon, he found that his Jeep was gone. The keys were still on his kitchen table, where he had left them this morning. The only other person who has access to his home is his live-in girlfriend, Cheryl J. Long, F/W, DOB: 5-26-1992, Ph. 920-738-5821. He contacted Cheryl, who said she did not take the Jeep. Cody is the sole owner of the Jeep; no one else is on the title. Cody did not give anyone permission to take or drive his vehicle.

Cody then checked the security video from the camera he has on the front of his house. It shows a subject, who initially approaches from East 27th Street (the intersection to the north of his home) entering his vehicle and driving away with it. He shows you the video:

Video: https://www.youtube.com/watch?v=J_WTx0xdvDI

After viewing the video, you check with all of Cody's neighbors on his block. You make contact with all the neighbors except for one: none of his neighbors saw anything related to this case. No one answered at 9148 Harbor Drive. When you ask Cody about this neighbor, he states that Tom Jenkins lives there. Cody says that Tom works second shift and was probably at work when you knocked at his door.

Incident # 18-51273-119

Field notes must be taken to gather the following information (at a minimum):

- Full information on complainant
- Full information on victim (if different than complainant)
- Full information on witness(es)

- Full information on suspect (if available)
- Description of entry, exit
- Description of items stolen/damaged
- Full description of vehicle, including who is on the title
- Nonconsent statement
- Evidence collected
- Was description of suspect/vehicle broadcast to the on-duty officers
- Stolen items/missing persons entered into NCIC

Suspect description protocol:

- Race/sex
- Approximate age
- Approximate height
- Approximate weight
- Hair length, style, and color
- Eye color (glasses worn—type)
- Clothing description (describe from head to toe)
- Name, or partial name, if known
- Scars, marks, tattoos
- Other characteristics (limp, stutter, braces on teeth, etc.)
- Associated vehicle

INCIDENT REPORT

Date:_____   Incident #_____

Nature of Incident:_____

Complainant:_____

Suspect:_____

Victim:_____

Witness #1:_____

Witness #2:_____

Witness #3:_____

Narrative:

_____

_____

_____

_____

_____

_____

_____

_____

_____

_____

_____

_____

_____

_____

_____

_____

_____

_____

_____

_____

_____

_____

_____

_____

_____

_____

_____

_____

_____

_____

_____

_____

_____

_____

_____

_____

_____

_____

_____

_____

_____

_____

Officer Signature _____

Officer Printed Name _____ Badge Number _____

EXERCISE 12: Motor Vehicle Theft

POLICE REPORT WRITING
Exercise 12
Motor Vehicle Theft

RUBRIC

Requirement	Learner		Instructor	
	Included	Not Included	Included	Not Included
Student has reviewed the assignment scenario and the video segment.				
Associated Competency **CO 2:** Differentiate reports based on type and purpose.				
Squad and shift assignment have been recorded in student's field notes.				
Time of dispatch and nature of assignment have been recorded in student's field notes.				
Observations of the scene (upon arrival and throughout investigation) have been recorded in student's field notes.				
Student has conducted an interview of the complainant, and recorded all pertinent information in his or her field notes.				
Names of complainant, victim, witnesses, and suspect/arrestee have been recorded in student's field notes.				
Student has recorded a victim statement of nonconsent in his or her field notes.				

Student has recorded a description of the vehicle, to include an estimated $ value and the name of the victim's insurance company in his or her field notes.				
A detailed description of the suspect is included in the student's field notes. Suspect description followed protocol.				
Student has documented complainant's statement about location of the car keys in his or her field notes.				
Student has identified any associated evidence and documented it in field notes.				
Student has documented the disposition of any evidence that was collected.				
A photocopy of the student's field notes has been included with this assignment submission.				
Associated Competency **CO 3:** Demonstrate thorough preparation to develop a report.				
Student has documented his or her response to this assignment from beginning to end.				
Narrative contains detailed, chronological descriptions of officer actions and observations.				
Squad and shift assignment have been recorded in student's report narrative.				
Time of dispatch and nature of assignment have been recorded in student's report narrative.				

Observations of the scene (upon arrival and throughout investigation) have been recorded in student's report narrative.				
Student has conducted an interview of the complainant, and recorded all pertinent information in his or her report narrative.				
Names of complainant, victim, witnesses, and suspect/arrestee have been recorded in student's report narrative.				
Student has recorded a victim statement of nonconsent in his or her report narrative.				
Student has recorded a description of the vehicle, to include an estimated $ value and the name of the victim's insurance company in his or her report narrative.				
A detailed description of the suspect is included in the student's report narrative. Suspect description followed protocol.				
Student has documented complainant's statement about location of the car keys in report narrative.				
Student has articulated facts that meet statutory elements in the report narrative.				
Student has identified any associated evidence and documented it in report narrative.				
Student has documented the disposition of any evidence that was collected.				
Venue in which incident occurred has been articulated in student's report narrative.				

Associated Competency **CO 4:** Construct a narrative report in a chronological format.				
Submission is formatted as follows: 1. Student-completed rubric 2. Narrative report with student name, date, type of report, and incident # typed in a block in the upper right corner of page 1 of the report 3. Photocopy of student field notes				
The report is clear, legible, and free of errors or stray marks.				
The report evidences correct grammar, punctuation, spelling, and sentence structure.				
Associated Competency **CO 7:** Edit reports for compliance with associated rules of grammar and syntax.				
Learner has ensured that all elements of the rubric have been fulfilled and the deadline for this report has been met.				

EXERCISE 13A

BURGLARY REPORT

Instructions: Read the scenario. Upon completion of your field notes, write a detailed offense report documenting what was reported and the details of your investigation.

On Monday, January 15, 2018, at 4:46 pm you are called to respond to 2169 Evergreen Drive, Green Bay, WI for a Burglary complaint. Upon arrival, you are met by Jerry C. Lindstrom, white / male, DOB: 05-09-65, of 2169 Evergreen Drive, Green Bay, WI 54307, Ph. (920)738-4142, who said that while he was at work at Goodman's Auto Mart, unknown person(s) entered his home and caused damage. He also explained that his wife, Jean T. Lindstrom, who is a stay-at-home-mom was gone. Lindstrom said that when he left for work, at 7:00 am, Jean was at home, folding laundry. When he returned home at approximately 4:15 pm, he discovered that she was missing. Lindstrom also reported that about a ½ hour before your arrival, an unknown male phoned him on his home landline and demanded $80,000 in exchange for his wife. The unknown male put Jean on the phone and she pled for help from Jerry. Jerry said that he and Jean have a 10-year-old son, William (Billy) K. Lindstrom, white / male, 02-27-08, who Jerry dropped off at Kennedy Elementary School on his way to work. Jerry also picked Billy up from school today on his way home from work (prior to discovering the burglary). After taking Lindstrom's statement, you notify your shift commander, Captain Riley Caldwell, who informs you that he will be sending a detective unit to your location. At approximately 6:17 pm Detective Sqd. 803 (Detectives Arlen and Calmes) arrive at the residence and, after you brief them, they explain that they will handle the kidnapping report, but you will be required to take the burglary complaint.

As a result, you check with a neighbor at 2171 Evergreen Drive. Rob S. Tomlinson, white / male, DOB: 04-14-70, answered the door and explained that he lives alone and was at work during the timeframe of the burglary. After interviewing Tomlinson, you knocked at the door of 2173 Evergreen Drive, but receive no answer. You then check across the street at 2168 Evergreen Drive, the home of Elaine P. Samuels, black / female, DOB: 10-23-49, Ph. (920)863-2112. She explained that she and her husband, Andrew, are both retired. While Andrew was taking a nap, at approximately 11:30 am, she (Elaine) saw a mid-1980s model, tan, 4-dr. sedan pull into the driveway of 2169 Evergreen Drive. Two white men got out of the car and approached the house. Both appeared to be in their mid-30s. One was thin with dark, receding hair. The other was taller and stockier, with blond hair that covered his ears. The thinner man was wearing a brown, waist-length suede jacket and rust-colored pants. The stockier man was wearing a dark brown leather trenchcoat.

Elaine said that she assumed they were servicemen whom Jean had called. Elaine reported seeing no other unusual circumstances at the Lindstrom's today. You also talk to Andrew C. Samuels, b/m, 8-28-45, who said that he woke up with a head cold and went back to bed at 10:00 am. He said he slept until 3:00 pm and did not see or hear anything unusual happening at the Lindstrom's. Next, you check with the neighbors at 2167 Evergreen Drive, but you are told by Wendy H. Cordell, w/f, 02-01-79, of 2165 Evergreen Drive, Ph. (920)738-5934, that the Hensons (Carrie and Roy) live at that address, but they left, approximately 2 weeks ago for their winter home in Arizona and that they won't be returning until April 2018. Cordell said that her husband, John Cordell, has been in Atlanta, Georgia, at a business conference for the last two days and won't return for two more days. She also said that, although she had been home all day, she had neither seen nor heard anyone at the Lindstrom's. Finally, you check with the neighbor to the rear of the Lindstrom's, Jackson T. Billings III, b/m, 11-07-81, of 2158 Carrington Way, Green Bay, WI 54307, Ph. (920)738-6647. Billings said that he and his wife Ariel (who was not home at the time) are both accounting professionals and were at work, downtown, during the day.

Prior to checking with the neighbors, you contacted Wade R. Goodman, owner of Goodman's Auto Mart. He confirmed that Jerry arrived at work at 7:30 am and did not leave until 4:30 pm.

A check of the area revealed two sets of boot impressions: one distinguishable, size 12, Rocky impression, left in the 2 inches of snow, on the deck in front of the living room window; and one size 9, Sorrell impression in 2 inches of snow on the stoop to the front door of the residence. Utilizing your evidence collection kit, you photograph the shoe prints and then lift plaster impressions. You observe tool pry marks on the front door jamb. There is also a brownish/red smear mark on the door jamb. There are brownish/red drops leading from the front door to the upstairs bathroom. In the upstairs bathroom, the curtain and rod are down, lying disheveled on the floor. There is also a basket of toiletries overturned on the counter, with the contents spilled over the vanity. There is also a brownish/red smudge on the vanity. You dust for prints and discover a readable latent print on an antibiotic tube located on the upstairs bathroom floor. You collect samples of the brownish/red smears as possible blood evidence, as well as collecting the latent print on the antibiotic tube. Prior to collecting any evidence, you photograph the entire scene.

Incident # 18-6319-876

Field notes must be taken to gather the following information, at a minimum:

- Full information on complainant
- Full information on victim, if different
- Description of entry, exit
- Description of items stolen/damaged
- Nonconsent statement
- Evidence collected
- Stolen items/missing persons entered into NCIC

Suspect description protocol:

- Race/sex
- Approximate age
- Approximate height
- Approximate weight
- Hair length, style, and color
- Eye color (glasses worn—type)
- Clothing description (describe from head to toe)
- Name, or partial name, if known
- Scars, marks, tattoos
- Other characteristics (limp, stutter, braces on teeth, etc.)
- Associated vehicle

INCIDENT REPORT

Date:_____   Incident #_____

Nature of Incident:_____

Complainant:_____

Suspect:_____

Victim:_____

Witness #1:_____

Witness #2:_____

Witness #3:_____

Narrative:

_____

_____

_____

_____

_____

_____

_____

_____

_____

_____

_____

_____

_____

_____

_____

_____

_____

_____

_____

_____

_____

_____

_____

_____

_____

_____

_____

_____

_____

_____

_____

_____

_____

_____

_____

_____

_____

_____

_____

_____

_____

Officer Signature _____

Officer Printed Name _____ Badge Number _____

POLICE REPORT WRITING
Exercise 13A
Burglary

RUBRIC

Requirement	Learner		Instructor	
	Included	Not Included	Included	Not Included
Student has reviewed the assignment scenario describing a burglary scene in preparation for completing this exercise.				
Associated Competency **CO 2:** Differentiate reports based on type and purpose.				
Squad and shift assignment have been recorded in student's field notes.				
Time of dispatch and nature of assignment have been recorded in student's field notes.				
Observations of the scene (upon arrival and throughout investigation) have been recorded in student's field notes.				
Student has conducted an interview of the complainant, and recorded all pertinent information in his or her field notes.				
Names of complainant, victim, witnesses, and suspect/arrestee have been recorded in student's field notes.				
Student has recorded a victim statement of nonconsent in his or her field notes.				
Student has recorded a description of damage or items taken, to include an estimated $ value of loss and the name of the victim's insurance company in his or her field notes.				

A detailed description of the suspect is included in the student's field notes. Suspect description followed protocol.				
Student has identified any associated evidence and documented it in field notes.				
Student has documented the disposition of any evidence that was collected.				
A photocopy of the student's field notes has been included with this assignment submission.				
Associated Competency **CO 3:** Demonstrate thorough preparation to develop a report.				
Student has documented his or her response to this assignment from beginning to end.				
Narrative contains detailed, chronological descriptions of officer actions and observations.				
Squad and shift assignment have been recorded in student's report narrative.				
Time of dispatch and nature of assignment have been recorded in student's report narrative.				
Observations of the scene (upon arrival and throughout investigation) have been recorded in student's report narrative.				
Student has conducted an interview of the complainant, and recorded all pertinent information in his or her report narrative.				
Names of complainant, victim, witnesses, and suspect/arrestee have been recorded in the student's report narrative.				

Student has recorded a victim statement of nonconsent in his or her report narrative.				
Student has recorded a description of damage or items taken, to include an estimated $ value of loss and the name of the victim's insurance company in his or her report narrative.				
A detailed description of the suspect is included in the student's report narrative. Suspect description followed protocol.				
Student has identified any associated evidence and documented it in the report narrative.				
Student has documented the disposition of any evidence that was collected.				
Venue in which incident occurred has been articulated in student's report narrative.				
Student has articulated any need for follow-up investigation in the concluding paragraph of the report narrative.				
Associated Competency **CO 4:** Construct a narrative report in a chronological format.				
Submission is formatted as follows: 1. Student-completed rubric 2. Narrative report with student name, date, type of report, and incident # typed in a block in the upper right corner of page 1 of the report 3. Photocopy of student field notes				
The report is clear, legible, and free of errors or stray marks.				
The report evidences correct grammar, punctuation, spelling, and sentence structure.				

SUPPLEMENT TO A BURGLARY REPORT

Instructions: Read the scenario. Upon completion of your field notes, write a detailed offense report documenting what was reported and the details of your investigation.

Scenario: On Monday, January 15, 2018, at 4:46 pm you were called to respond to 2169 Evergreen Drive, Green Bay, WI for a Burglary complaint. On that date, relative to your initial investigation, you made an attempt to interview a neighbor at 2173 Evergreen Drive regarding any observation of suspicious activity or suspects in the area within the timeframe of the burglary. During that attempt you received no answer. On Tuesday, January 16, 2018, at 5:53 pm, you returned to 2173 Evergreen Drive and spoke to the resident, Candace Reynolds, b/f, 03-14-1986, Ph. (920)847-2370, who said that she was home during the timeframe of the burglary occurrence because she had taken off of work to clean her house in preparation for a visit from her sister, later in the day. Reynolds said that she had been on her way to the airport to get her sister when you made your initial attempt to contact her. Candace explained that at about lunchtime (approximately 12:00 noon), on 01-15-18, she heard some loud voices, both male, having what sounded like an argument. She was unable to distinguish anything that was said, but the sound caused her to glance out of her side window where she saw a tan, 4-door car backing out of the driveway at the Lindstrom's. The car then drove down the block and out of view (away from the direction of her house). She said that she did not get a good look at the people in the car and couldn't tell whether they were male or female. She just assumed that they were both men because of the voices she had heard seconds before. Prior to leaving 2173 Evergreen Drive, you spoke with Janice Davis, b/f, 7-19-1988, of 37 Fawn Dr., Atlanta, Georgia 30341 (Candace's sister) who confirmed that Candace had picked her up at the airport at approximately 4:30 pm on January 15, 2018. You then left your business card with Candace so that she could contact you with further information, should she recall any. After the end of your interview, you compose a supplemental report to document Reynolds's statement.

SUPPLEMENTAL REPORT

Date:_____   Incident #_____

Narrative:

_____

_____

_____

_____

_____

_____

_____

_____

_____

_____

_____

_____

_____

_____

_____

_____

_____

_____

_____

_____

_____

_____

_____

_____

_____

_____

_____

_____

_____

_____

_____

_____

_____

_____

_____

_____

_____

_____

_____

_____

_____

_____

_____

_____

_____

_____

_____

_____

_____

_____

_____

_____

_____

_____

_____

_____

_____

_____

Officer Signature _____

Officer Printed Name _____ Badge Number _____

POLICE REPORT WRITING
Exercise 13B
Supplement to a Burglary Report

RUBRIC

Requirement	Learner		Instructor	
	Included	Not Included	Included	Not Included
Student has reviewed the assignment scenario from Exercises 13a and 13b in preparation for completing this exercise.				
Associated Competency **CO 2:** Differentiate reports based on type and purpose.				
Time of arrival at the witness address has been recorded in student's field notes.				
Student has conducted an interview of the witness, and recorded all pertinent information in his or her field notes.				
Names witness(es) or other pertinent contacts have been recorded in the student's field notes.				
A detailed description of suspect information is included in the student's field notes.				
Student has identified any associated evidence and documented it in field notes.				
A photocopy of the student's field notes has been included with this assignment submission.				
Associated Competency **CO 3:** Demonstrate thorough preparation to develop a report.				

Squad and shift assignment have been recorded in student's report narrative.			
Time of arrival at the witness address has been recorded in the student's report narrative.			
Student has conducted an interview of the witness, and recorded all pertinent information in his or her report narrative.			
Names of witness(es) or other pertinent contacts have been recorded in student's report narrative.			
A detailed description of suspect information is included in the student's report narrative.			
Student has articulated any need for further follow-up investigation in the concluding paragraph of the report narrative.			
Associated Competency **CO 4:** Construct a narrative report in a chronological format.			
Submission is formatted as follows: 1. Student-completed rubric 2. Narrative report with student name, date, type of report, and incident # typed in a block in the upper right corner of page 1 of the report 3. Photocopy of student field notes			
The report is clear, legible, and free of errors or stray marks.			
Associated Competency **CO 7:** Edit reports for compliance with associated rules of grammar and syntax.			
The report evidences correct grammar, punctuation, spelling, and sentence structure.			

SEARCH WARRANT AFFIDAVIT

Instructions: Read the scenario. Upon completion of your field notes, complete the search warrant affidavit.

Complaint: Possession, With Intent to Deliver a Controlled Substance (Cocaine)

Incident # 18-7571-643

Scenario: On Friday, January 26, 2018, at 4:15 pm, you were approached by your supervisor, Lieutenant James Atkinson, who assigned you to investigate the activities at 1307 N. 49th St. in the City of Green Bay. Lt. Atkinson gave you a number of anonymous citizen complaints which articulated activities consistent with use and delivery of a controlled substance, specifically, cocaine. These activities included people openly smoking cocaine base (commonly referred to as crack) on the porch of the residence in the evening hours (6 pm to midnight); a large volume of vehicular traffic, stopping for a couple of minutes at a time, the occupants of which approach the front door of the residence, make an exchange and leave the residence without ever entering.

As a result of receiving this assignment and information, you collected one full, white kitchen garbage bag, abandoned at the curb, in front of 1307 N. 49th St. at 2:47 am on Monday, January 29, 2018. You transported the trash back to the police station where you searched it and discovered an AT&T bill (postmarked 1-19-2018), a Home Depot advertisement, and a Wisconsin Public Services electric/gas bill (postmarked 1-17-2018), all in the name of Brian M. Shreve. Located in the same bag as the above listed identifiers was a sandwich bag containing a white powdery substance, consistent with the appearance of powder cocaine. You conducted a Narcopouch test of a sample of the white powdery residue from one of the sandwich bags and observed a positive reaction for cocaine. You also discovered the remnants of 20 wrinkled sandwich bags with the corners cut out of them. The identifiers were photocopied and the copies were attached to the incident report. The original identifying documents, the sandwich bags, and sandwich bag remnants were placed on evidence inventory #E-18-114751.

On Monday, February 5, 2018, at 3:17 am, you returned to 1307 N. 49th St. and, again, collected the trash, abandoned at the curb, in front of that address. The trash consisted of three white kitchen garbage bags. After transporting the trash to the police station, you searched bags 1 and 2 and discovered no identifiers and no evidence in either. Upon searching bag 3 you discovered a partially crushed Pepsi can with eight small holes poked in the middle (dented portion) and a black/discolored burn mark in the paint of the can around the area of the holes. You also discovered a ziptop freezer bag containing a white powdery substance. Also in bag 3, you found a Dentist bill (postmarked 1-24-2018), in the name of Brian M. Shreve, of 1307 N. 49th St. You also found a bill from American Family Insurance (postmarked 1-21-2018) and a March of Dimes donation envelope (postmarked 1-24-2018), both in the name of Brian M. Shreve. Upon conducting a Narcopouch field test of the white powdery substance from the ziptop bag, you received a positive indication for the presence of cocaine. You then inventoried the above evidence on inventory #E18-114943.

Department in-house records indicate that Brian M. Shreve, w/m, 12-24-90, of 1307 N. 49th St., Ph. (920)886-1147, has had numerous contacts with officers of your agency within the last 2 years, to include Possession of Cocaine, Battery, Resisting an Officer, Disorderly Conduct, Bail Jumping, and Issuance of Worthless Check. His most recent contact was for speeding on 12-27-17. His address of record for each one of the listed incidents was 1307 N. 49th St. In addition to checking in-house records, you also speak to one of your reliable confidential informants in the area who says that he knows Brian Shreve and has purchased "crack rocks" from him on at least three occasions since Thanksgiving.

On Monday, February 5, 2018, at 8:23 pm, you met with your confidential informant in the area of 1307 N. 49th St. You had the informant empty the contents of all of his pockets leaving the contents locked in his car. You then conducted a consent search of the informant, for contraband, weapons, and money. You found none of those things. You then gave the informant $15.00 which you vouchered from the police department. At 8:30 pm, you observed the informant ring the doorbell at 1307 N. 49th St. He then entered the residence. Your informant was there until 8:34 pm, when he returned to you with what appeared to be a knotted sandwich bag corner containing a hard, white, waxy chunk, similar in appearance to a fragment of white bar soap. Your informant said that he bought a "crack rock" directly from Brian Shreve. He further said that when he entered the home through the front door, Shreve was in the living room. He said that Shreve then entered a bedroom that was immediately off the living room, to the left. Your informant said that he could see into the bedroom from the living room and observed Shreve retrieving the "crack" from a shoe box, kept on the upper shelf of a closet. You return to the police station and test a small portion of the white waxy chunk by using a Narcopouch. The result of the test was "positive" for the presence of cocaine. The weight of the white, waxy chunk, in the original package was 0.2 gram. The white, waxy substance, in its original package, was then placed on evidence inventory #E12-115019.

On Tuesday, February 6, 2018, at approximately 1 pm, you conduct a surveillance of the residence at 1307 N. 49th St., to obtain a physical description of the residence.

Physical Description

1307 N. 49th St. is located in the City of Green Bay, Brown County, WI and is a single family, two-story house, located on the west side of N. 49th St. The front of the house faces east, toward 9th St. The house has light gray vinyl siding with white trim and a black shingled roof. There are two exterior doors to the residence. One is located on the eastern (front) wall. The other is on the western (rear) wall of the residence. There is a porch, leading up to the front door. The porch spans the entire width of the front of the house. When facing the front of the house, the front door is situated on the left side of the porch and is white in color and has a glass storm door over it. There are two small windows located in the top quarter portion of the door. The number "1307" is arranged diagonally (descending from left to right) on the wall on the right side of the front door.

Assignment Instructions

Using the Drug Affidavit Example (see Appendix B) for guidance, complete the Affidavit for Search Warrant for the above scenario. (Note: Boilerplate language is intentionally highlighted to distinguish it from case-specific information.)

CIRCUIT COURT BRANCH   BROWN COUNTY   STATE OF WISCONSIN

STATE OF WISCONSIN   AFFIDAVIT IN SUPPORT OF SEARCH WARRANT
(COUNTY OF BROWN)

      Deputy_____, a law enforcement officer of the Brown County Sheriff's Department, being duly sworn on oath, says that on this day in Brown County, in and upon certain premises in the City, Town, Village of _____, in said County, which premises are occupied or owned by persons named and unnamed including _____, and which premises are described as follows:

_____

_____

_____

_____

There are now located at and concealed therein certain things, which are:

1. Cocaine and other controlled substances.
2. Scales, bags, containers, and other items used in the manufacturing and delivery of controlled substances.
3. Ledgers, documents, phone numbers, tapes, pagers, cell phones, safes and their contents, and other instruments evidencing drug transactions.
4. US currency.
5. Weapons.

which things are possessed for the purpose of evading or violating the laws of the State of Wisconsin and contrary to Section 961.41 of the Wisconsin Statutes; and/or; which things were used in the commission of or may constitute the evidence of the crime of possession with intent to deliver committed in violation of Section 961.41 of the Wisconsin Statutes.

The facts tending to establish the grounds for issuing search warrant are as follows:

1. Deputy _____, being first duly sworn, on oath, deposes and says, that affiant relies for the issuance of this search warrant upon information and belief, based upon:

2. Deputy_____ is a ___-year veteran of the Brown County Sheriff's Department. He is presently assigned as a direct enforcement officer for the City, Town, Village of _____ for approximately _____ years. He has been trained in basic narcotic identification and field-testing controlled substances.

Based upon your affiant's training, experience, and participation in this and other narcotics investigations, and based upon the knowledge derived from other experienced officers with whom your affiant is associated, your Affiant knows that:

a. Persons dealing in controlled substances commonly keep a supply of the drug or drugs they sell on hand for immediate sale. These drugs are commonly kept on the trafficker's person, in their home, or in their vehicles. Traffickers typically store any large amounts of drugs in locked containers or security containers to protect their investment in the drugs. Often, the traffickers will hide their supply of controlled substances in garages, out buildings, storage areas and sheds associated with their premises, and by burying these substances in the ground to conceal the fact of the possession of the drugs.

b. Drug traffickers commonly package their products at their homes in such containers as plastic bags of various sizes, paper sacks, folded paper (referred to as bindles), cigarette papers, glass vials, film canisters, aluminum foil packets, envelopes and other similar containers. Prior to packaging the drugs, traffickers commonly use scales and other measuring devices to weigh controlled substances, which items would often contain residue of the drugs weighed or measured. The controlled substances commonly packaged or otherwise prepared by drug traffickers prior to delivery include, but are not limited to marijuana, hashish, opium, cocaine, cocaine base (crack), lysergic acid diethylamide (LSD), methamphetamines (crank), heroin, psilocybin (mushrooms), morphine, methcathinone (cat), and illegally obtained prescription drugs. Drug traffickers often possess various cutting agents, which are used to dilute controlled substances prior to distribution.

c. The traffickers of controlled substances are often themselves users of the drug or drugs they traffic. Controlled substances are ingested into the human body by being smoked, either by use of a hand-rolled cigarette or pipe; swallowed; snorted; or injected by needle and syringe. Paraphernalia for the use of controlled substances will often be found at the premises associated with drug traffickers. Users often maintain photographs and audio/video recordings of themselves and/or associates using controlled substances, displaying large sums of money, and/or indicating gang affiliation.

d. Those who traffic in controlled substances frequently keep records of such transactions, such as would be kept by a legitimate businessman engaged in the sale of legitimate goods. Such records include, but are not limited to: customer lists, price lists, notes of telephone messages, financial journals, bank accounts books and papers, notes of money owed, and records of past purchases of controlled substances. These records may exist in the form of actual documents or as data in a computer, cell phone address book or call list, or caller ID unit.

Drug traffickers generally acquire and utilize security, communications and counter surveillance equipment. Such equipment includes telephone pagers and mobile telephones (for the purpose of communicating with suppliers and customers), firearms and ammunition (for the purpose of protection against police raids, thefts of their property and rip-offs by suppliers or customers), and radio scanners (to monitor police radio channels).

e. People in general receive correspondence at their residences. Such correspondence usually includes, but is not limited to: telephone bills, utility bills, rental agreements, rent receipts, personal letters, photographs, and canceled mail envelopes. Such items tend to reflect the identification of persons in control of and having dominion over the residence, and, as such, the items will be found within the residence.

f. Drug traffickers frequently keep large sums of money on hand which represents the profits they make on the sale of their drugs and which is to be used for the purchase of more controlled substances or which may be used to facilitate their lifestyles. Larger sums of money are sometimes kept in locked containers or security containers or otherwise hidden upon the premises. Drug traffickers may also possess safety deposit boxes to hide their money, the existence of which may be made known by the discovery of keys or banking documents.

g. Drug traffickers often destroy evidence upon the arrival of police officers announcing the execution of a search warrant. These drug traffickers also often possess weapons for protection of their controlled substances against thieves and for use against police officers executing search warrants. As a result, the process of executing a drug search warrant is normally very dangerous. Therefore, police officers executing a drug search warrant must do so in a rapid and surprising manner to lessen the time available for drug traffickers to destroy evidence or obtain weapons.

h. Drugs traffickers obtain the drugs they sell from other sources, or the chemicals and substances needed to produce drugs from other sources. To obtain these substances, the drug traffickers or their agents (mules) will need to travel from one location to another and meet with the source of these substances. Drug traffickers and their agents will conduct these meetings in a covert manner, to avoid detection by the police. Vehicles owned by or utilized by the drug trafficker or agent will normally be used to facilitate these meetings, by transporting the parties to the meeting site, bringing purchase money for the substances to be obtained, and transporting the substances obtained. Drug traffickers will also use rental cars and low value cars to thwart efforts of law enforcement and possibly foil asset forfeiture actions.

i. A "Drug house" or Drug Trafficking Place can be a residence, business, hotel room, car, boat or similar location or conveyance. A Drug Trafficking Place is best described as a place where drugs are stored and/or a place from which drugs are distributed and/or as a place where drugs are used. Whether a "Drug House" is a place of distribution or a secluded place where people go to use controlled substances, both have certain common elements. Both types of places are engaged in an illegal activity which attracts and is commonly frequented by users of controlled substances. Generally, all persons present including persons not residing at the location, are likely to be there in connection to the illegal activity and therefore are likely to possess controlled substances, drug paraphernalia or money either intended to purchase controlled substances or as proceeds from the sale of controlled substances. WI Statute 968.16 clearly permits officers to search all persons present at the time of the warrants execution. However, in certain instances officers must first establish a reasonable connection between the person and the illegal activity before proceeding with a search of their person or property on their person.

3._____

_____

_____

_____

4.

5._____

_____

_____

_____

_____

_____

_____

_____

_____

_____

_____

_____

_____

_____

Wherefore, the said Deputy _____, a law enforcement officer, prays that a search warrant be issued to search such premises for the said property, and if found, to seize the same and take the property into custody according to law.

_____

Affiant - Law Enforcement Officer

Subscribed and sworn to before me this

_____ day of _____ , _____.

Honorable _____   Honorable _____

JUDGE OF CIRCUIT COURT BRANCH ___   OR COURT COMMISSIONER

BROWN COUNTY, WISCONSIN   CIRCUIT COURT BRANCH ___

BROWN COUNTY, WISCONSIN

POLICE REPORT WRITING
Exercise 14A
Search Warrant Affidavit

RUBRIC

Requirement	Learner		Instructor	
	Included	Not Included	Included	Not Included
Associated Competency **CO 2:** Differentiate reports based on type and purpose.				
Student has completed an affidavit for a search warrant to include all of the following elements:				
Associated Competency **CO 3:** Demonstrate thorough preparation to develop a report.				
Detailed, chronological descriptions of officer actions and observations				
Reasonable suspicion to investigate further				
Work done to establish probable cause that the offense has been, or is occurring				
Evidence of the identification of the primary resident(s)				
Detailed description of the residence to be searched				
Venue (city and county) of the offense has been properly documented in the narrative.				
Report follows the format for a Search Warrant Affidavit.				

Submission is formatted as follows: 1. Student-completed rubric 2. Completed Search Warrant Affidavit				
Associated Competency **CO 4:** Construct a narrative report in a chronological format.				
The report is clear, legible, and free of errors or stray marks.				
The report evidences correct grammar, punctuation, spelling, and sentence structure.				
Associated Competency **CO 7:** Edit reports for compliance with associated rules of grammar and syntax.				
Learner has ensured that all elements of the rubric have been fulfilled and the deadline for this report has been met.				

EXERCISE 14B

SEARCH WARRANT RETURN REPORT

Instructions: The student will write a categorical report narrative describing which articles of evidence were discovered in which of the listed areas of the house. The student may decide the location of each of the evidentiary articles, but at least one article should have been discovered in each area.

The search warrant that was issued relative to the affidavit (developed in Exercise 14a) has yielded the collection of a variety of types of evidence. Articles of evidence were discovered in six different locations in the house: living room, southwest bedroom, southeast (master) bedroom, master bathroom, kitchen, and basement (northeast corner). The evidence discovered during warrant execution included:

- 1—Ohaus brand triple beam scale
- 21—plastic sandwich bags containing white, powdery residue (missing one lower corner each)
- 17—plastic bag corners each containing a white, powdery, crystalline substance (tied with a knot)
- 1—ledger containing notes on product quantities, volume, price, and sales
- 45—3" X 3" squares of white paper (possibly used to make pharmaceutical folds [bindles])
- $3000.00 in cash (all in $100.00 bills)
- 1—Smith and Wesson model 586, .357 cal. revolver, stainless steel finish, 6" barrel, Ser. # 586sw418753
- 1—Ball brand mason jar containing stems and seeds
- 1—1 gallon Glad freezer bag containing 18 oz. of a green, leafy substance
- 10—sandwich bags containing a green, leafy substance
- 1—Remington Model 870, 12 gauge, pump action shotgun, blue steel finish, sawed-off barrel, Ser. # 9981346780
- 1—Beretta Model 70, .22 cal. semi-automatic pistol, blue steel finish, 2.5" barrel, Ser. # Ber471399176
- 1—32 oz. plastic jar of "Mannitol" (white powdery dietary supplement)
- 1—Samsung Galaxy S6 cell phone
- 3—glass pipes with charred residue in the bowls
- 4—metal pipes with charred residue in the bowls
- 7—alligator clips with charred residue on the sides
- 4—pipe screens with charred residue on each
- 1—package of partially used "Chore Boy" brand scouring pad
- 13—charred "Chore Boy" plugs

SUPPLEMENTAL REPORT

Date:_____   Incident #_____

Narrative:

_____

_____

_____

_____

_____

_____

_____

_____

_____

_____

_____

_____

_____

_____

_____

_____

_____

_____

_____

_____

_____

_____

_____

_____

_____

_____

_____

_____

_____

_____

_____

_____

_____

_____

_____

_____

_____

_____

_____

_____

_____

_____

_____

_____

_____

_____

Officer Signature _____

Officer Printed Name _____ Badge Number _____

POLICE REPORT WRITING
Exercise 14B
Search Warrant Return Report

RUBRIC

Requirement	Learner		Instructor	
	Included	Not Included	Included	Not Included
Associated Competency **CO 2:** Differentiate reports based on type and purpose.				
Student has completed a Search Warrant Return report.				
Associated Competency **CO 3:** Demonstrate thorough preparation to develop a report.				
Search Warrant Return report must include the following elements:				
Incident # associated with the drug investigation that generated the search warrant				
Date, time, and location of warrant execution				
Name(s) and unit number(s) of officer(s) executing the warrant				
Detailed description of the residence that was searched (consistent with description in Exercise 14A)				
Detailed description of areas where evidence was discovered				
Detailed list of articles discovered in each respective area of the house				
Name(s) and unit number(s) of officer(s) collecting and inventorying the evidence				

Location of where the evidence is being securely stored				
Date and time of evidentiary inventory, along with inventory number				
Associated Competency **CO 4:** Construct a narrative report in a chronological format.				
Submission is formatted as follows: 1. Student-completed rubric 2. Completed Search Warrant Affidavit				
Associated Competency **CO 5:** Construct a narrative report in a categorical format.				
The report is clear, legible, and free of errors or stray marks.				
The report evidences correct grammar, punctuation, spelling, and sentence structure.				
Associated Competency **CO 7:** Edit reports for compliance with associated rules of grammar and syntax.				
Learner has ensured that all elements of the rubric have been fulfilled and the deadline for this report has been met.				

APPENDIX A

COURSE COMPETENCIES

Competency 1: Describe the purpose of police reports.
  Learning Objective 1: Identify various users/readers of police reports.

Competency 2: Differentiate reports based on type and purpose.
  Learning Objective 1: Describe various types of reports.
  Learning Objective 2: Contrast structural components of various types of reports.

Competency 3: Demonstrate thorough preparation to develop a report.
  Learning Objective 1: Utilize structured note-taking techniques.
  Learning Objective 2: Employ a standardized format for gathering basic information.
  Learning Objective 3: Engage in a note-taking process.
  Learning Objective 4: Contrast the types of information to be gathered.
  Learning Objective 5: Exhibit consistency in note-taking.
  Learning Objective 6: Plan the structure of the report.
  Learning Objective 7: Recognize the audience that the report is being written for.

Competency 4: Construct a narrative report in a chronological format.
  Learning Objective 1: Distinguish between chronological and categorical formats.
  Learning Objective 2: Develop an introduction that identifies the author, nature and time frame of the report.
  Learning Objective 3: Create a sequentially arranged body of the report.
  Learning Objective 4: Arrange subtopics and events by paragraph.
  Learning Objective 5: Articulate presence of criminal elements when applicable.
  Learning Objective 6: Identify venue in which the associated incident occurred.
  Learning Objective 7: Describe features of property, locations, and individuals through the use of physical characteristics.
  Learning Objective 8: Explain case disposition, investigative status, and follow-up necessities in a conclusion section.

Competency 5: Construct a narrative report in a categorical format.

    Learning Objective 1: Distinguish between chronological and categorical formats.

    Learning Objective 2: Identify categories/subcategories to be described within the report.

    Learning Objective 3: Arrange categories/subcategories by paragraph.

    Learning Objective 4: Describe features of property, locations, and individuals through the use of physical characteristics.

    Learning Objective 5: Explain case disposition, investigative status, and follow-up when applicable.

Competency 6: Improve the quality of a report through revision of a previous draft.

    Learning Objective 1: Screen a report draft for accuracy, validity, and consistency.

    Learning Objective 2: Recognize wordy content.

    Learning Objective 3: Modify content to be concise.

    Learning Objective 4: Develop report with regard for the associated users.

Competency 7: Edit reports for compliance with associated rules of grammar and syntax.

    Learning Objective 1: Recognize improper application of grammar and syntax.

    Learning Objective 2: Apply appropriate grammar and syntax to all sentences within the narrative.

Competency 8: Perform final review prior to report submission.

    Learning Objective 1: Proofread report for adherence to fundamental concepts of narrative report writing.

Competency 9: Develop a supplemental narrative report.

    Learning Objective 1: Identify information that should be included in a supplemental narrative report.

Competency 10: Dispose of field notes appropriately.

    Learning Objective 1: Identify associated policies regarding retention/disposal of field notes.

    Learning Objective 2: Articulate preservation of field notes within report when applicable.

APPENDIX B

SEARCH WARRANT AFFIDAVIT EXAMPLE

CIRCUIT COURT BRANCH   BROWN COUNTY   STATE OF WISCONSIN

STATE OF WISCONSIN)

) SS   AFFIDAVIT IN SUPPORT OF SEARCH WARRANT

COUNTY OF BROWN   )

    Deputy Daniel Sandford, a law enforcement officer of the Brown County Sheriff's Department, being duly sworn on oath, says that on this day in Brown County, in and upon certain premises in the Village of Allouez, in said County, which premises are occupied or owned by persons named and unnamed including Rita M. Camden, Arthur A. Davidson and Mark W. Coles, and which premises are described as follows:

    930 Derby Lane is a two story, one family house, with a detached garage on the southeast side. It is a white house with white trim and black shutters on the residence. The black numbers 930 are located on the north side of the residence next to the front door on the porch. To include in and around the garage are vehicles owned or operated by tenants or occupants of 930 Derby Lane and specifically including:

    A gold 2006 Chevy Cobalt four door sedan bearing WI registration of 131-MLV and VIN#1G1AK55F167731618, registered to Joseph F. Coles, 06-10-67 or Rose M. Coles, 09-05-68 at 1114 Westlawn Dr., DePere, WI 54115.

    There are now located at and concealed therein certain things, which are:

1. Marijuana and other controlled substances.
2. Scales, bags, containers, and other items used in the manufacturing and delivery of controlled substances.
3. Ledgers, documents, phone numbers, tapes, pagers, cell phones, safes and their contents, and other instruments evidencing drug transactions.
4. US currency.
5. Weapons.

which things are possessed for the purpose of evading or violating the laws of the State of Wisconsin and contrary to Section 961.41 of the Wisconsin Statutes; and/or; which things were used in the commission of or may constitute the evidence of the crime of possession with intent to deliver committed in violation of Section 961.41 of the Wisconsin Statutes.

The facts tending to establish the grounds for issuing search warrant are as follows:

1.   Deputy Daniel Sandford, being first duly sworn, on oath, deposes and says, that affiant relies for the issuance of this search warrant upon information and belief, based upon:

2.   Deputy Daniel Sandford is a 13-year veteran of the Brown County Sheriff's Department. He is presently assigned as a direct enforcement officer for the Village of Allouez for approximately four years. He has been trained in basic narcotic identification and field-testing controlled substances.

Based upon your affiant's training, experience, and participation in this and other narcotics investigations, and based upon the knowledge derived from other experienced officers with whom your affiant is associated, your Affiant knows that:

a. Persons dealing in controlled substances commonly keep a supply of the drug or drugs they sell on hand for immediate sale. These drugs are commonly kept on the trafficker's person, in their home, or in their vehicles. Traffickers typically store any large amounts of drugs in locked containers or security containers to protect their investment in the drugs. Often, the traffickers will hide their supply of controlled substances in garages, out buildings, storage areas and sheds associated with their premises, and by burying these substances in the ground to conceal the fact of the possession of the drugs.

b. Drug traffickers commonly package their products at their homes in such containers as plastic bags of various sizes, paper sacks, folded paper (referred to as bindles), cigarette papers, glass vials, film canisters, aluminum foil packets, envelopes and other similar containers. Prior to packaging the drugs, traffickers commonly use scales and other measuring devices to weigh controlled substances, which items would often contain residue of the drugs weighed or measured. The controlled substances commonly packaged or otherwise prepared by drug traffickers prior to delivery include, but are not limited to marijuana, hashish, opium, cocaine, cocaine base (crack), lysergic acid diethalmide (LSD), methamphetamines (crank), heroin, psilocybin (mushrooms), morphine, methcathedone (cat), and illegally obtained prescription drugs. Drug traffickers often possess various cutting agents, which are used to dilute controlled substances prior to distribution.

c. The traffickers of controlled substances are often themselves users of the drug or drugs they traffic. Controlled substances are ingested into the human body by being smoked, either by use of a hand-rolled cigarette or pipe; swallowed; snorted; or injected by needle and syringe. Paraphernalia for the use of controlled substances will often be found at the premises associated with drug traffickers. Users often maintain photographs and audio/video recordings of themselves and/or associates using controlled substances, displaying large sums of money, and/or indicating gang affiliation.

d. Those who traffic in controlled substances frequently keep records of such transactions, such as would be kept by a legitimate businessman engaged in the sale of legitimate goods. Such records include, but are not limited to: customer lists, price lists, notes of telephone messages, financial journals, bank accounts books and papers, notes of money owed, and records of past purchases of controlled substances. These records may exist in the form of actual documents or as data in a computer, cell phone address book or call list, or caller ID unit.

e. Drug traffickers generally acquire and utilize security, communications and counter surveillance equipment. Such equipment includes telephone pagers and mobile telephones (for the purpose of communicating with suppliers and customers), firearms and ammunition (for the purpose of protection against police raids, thefts of their property and rip-offs by suppliers or customers), and radio scanners (to monitor police radio channels).

f. People in general receive correspondence at their residences. Such correspondence usually includes, but is not limited to: telephone bills, utility bills, rental agreements, rent receipts, personal letters, photographs, and canceled mail envelopes. Such items tend to reflect the identification of persons in control of and having dominion over the residence, and, as such, the items will be found within the residence.

g. Drug traffickers frequently keep large sums of money on hand which represents the profits they make on the sale of their drugs and which is to be used for the purchase of more controlled substances or which may be used to facilitate their lifestyles. Larger sums of money are sometimes kept in locked containers or security containers or otherwise hidden upon the premises. Drug traffickers may also possess safety deposit boxes to hide their money, the existence of which may be made known by the discovery of keys or banking documents.

h. Drug traffickers often destroy evidence upon the arrival of police officers announcing the execution of a search warrant. These drug traffickers also often possess weapons for protection of their controlled substances against thieves and for use against police officers executing search warrants. As a result, the process of executing a drug search warrant is normally very dangerous. Therefore, police officers executing a drug search warrant must do so in a rapid and surprising manner to lessen the time available for drug traffickers to destroy evidence or obtain weapons.

i. Drugs traffickers obtain the drugs they sell from other sources, or the chemicals and substances needed to produce drugs from other sources. To obtain these substances, the drug traffickers or their agents (mules) will need to travel from one location to another and meet with the source of these substances. Drug traffickers and their agents will conduct these meetings in a covert manner, to avoid detection by the police. Vehicles owned by or utilized by the drug trafficker or agent will normally be used to facilitate these meetings, by transporting the parties to the meeting site, bringing purchase money for the substances to be obtained, and transporting the substances obtained. Drug traffickers will also use rental cars and low value cars to thwart efforts of law enforcement and possibly foil asset forfeiture actions.

j. A "Drug house" or Drug Trafficking Place can be a residence, business, hotel room, car, boat or similar location or conveyance. A Drug Trafficking Place is best described as a place where drugs are stored and/or a place from which drugs are distributed and/or as a place where drugs are used. Whether a "Drug House" is a place of distribution or a secluded place where people go to use controlled substances, both have certain common elements. Both types of places are engaged in an illegal activity which attracts and is commonly frequented by users of controlled substances. Generally, all persons present including persons not residing at the location, are likely to be there in connection to the illegal activity and therefore are likely to possess controlled substances, drug paraphernalia or money either intended to purchase controlled substances or as proceeds from the sale of controlled substances. WI Statute 968.16 clearly permits officers to search all persons present at the time of the warrants execution. However, in certain instances officers must first establish a reasonable connection between the person and the illegal activity before proceeding with a search of their person or property on their person.

3.   In January of 2009, your affiant received tip information from the Brown County Drug Task Force that there was suspicious short-term traffic during late night hours at 2903 Kirby Lane. The Drug Task Force stated that one of the residents of 2903 Kirby Lane, Rose Camden, was a suspect in a prior drug case in 2008. On January 8th and January 15th, 2009, Deputy N. Stevens conducted traffic stops on vehicles leaving 2903 Kirby Lane and he arrested subjects on warrants and controlled substance violations on both days. Deputy Flannery advised your affiant that he arrested a subject during the same period for warrants and the subject stated that a man named Coles was dealing marijuana out of the residence at 2903 Kirby Lane. Due to the drug history of Rose Camden, vehicle traffic from the residence, and the continued suspicious activity at 2903 Kirby Lane your affiant believed an investigation was appropriate.

4.   On 01-19-09 at approximately 7:15 am, your affiant conducted an abandoned refuse examination of the contents of the plastic garbage bin, utilized by the Village of Allouez, located at the curb in front of 2903 Kirby Lane. Five bags of garbage were located in the bin and three bags were lying next to the bin. Five of the garbage bags were consistent in size and color with each other and were black with a red tie. The other three bags were consistent in size and color and were black in color with no tie off. In bag 1 your affiant found the twisted and torn off corner of a baggie, 1.4 grams of green plantlike material consistent with marijuana stems and seeds that your affiant tested using the #8 Duquenois Reagent field test and it showed a positive result for the presence of THC. Your affiant also found four cigar blunts with burnt residue weighing 0.9 gram. In bag 2, your affiant found a check from Virtual Lending Source to Arthur Davidson, 0.7 gram of green plant stems and seeds, twisted and torn off corner of a baggie and a baggie with the corner torn off and missing. In bag 4 your affiant found 0.8 gram of green plant stems and seeds, four baggies tied in knots with the corners torn off and missing, and three twisted off baggie corners. In bag 5 your affiant found an empty plastic soda bottle with an aluminum foil wrapped cigar with burnt residue. Your affiant tested the residue in the cigar with the #8 Duquenois Reagent field test and it showed a positive result for the presence of THC. Your affiant also found a letter from the Humane Society addressed to William James at 2903 Kirby Lane, 0.8 gram of green plant stems, two twisted off baggie corners, two cigar blunts with burnt residue weighing 0.7 gram, and a baggie of green plantlike material consistent with marijuana that your affiant tested using the #8 Duquenois Reagent field test and it showed a positive result for the presence of THC. I observed loose tobacco, swisher sweet cigar boxes, and blunt wrappers in at least five of the eight garbage bags. Nothing of evidentiary value was found in bags 3, 6, or 7. All evidence collected was processed and placed into evidence at the Brown County Sheriff's Department. Your affiant tested evidence using the #8 Duquenois Reagent field test and it showed a positive result for the presence of THC in all evidence tested.

5.   On 02-02-09 at approximately 7:10 am, your affiant conducted an abandoned refuse examination of the contents of the plastic garbage bin, utilized by the Village of Allouez, located at the curb in front of 2903 Kirby Lane. Seven bags of garbage were located in the bin and three bags were lying next to the bin. In bag 7 your affiant found four torn off baggie corners, three tied off baggies missing corners, 0.6 gram of green plantlike stems and seeds, and the end of a blunt with burnt residue. In bag 8 your affiant found an OWI responsible party form with the names Mark Coles and Rose Camden and a Walgreen's prescription to Rose Camden. In bag 9 your affiant found a tied off baggie missing a corner, a Capital One bill for

Arthur Davidson, a letter addressed to Rose Camden from the University of Green Bay, a 1st Financial Bank statement addressed to Rose Camden, and a handwritten receipt note for rent at 2903 Kirby Lane. I observed loose tobacco in bags 7 and 8. Bags 1 thru 10 were consistent in the same size and color except for bag 4. Bag 4 was a black plastic bag with a red tie. Bags 1 thru 3 and 4 thru 10 were a black plastic bag with no tie. Bags 1 thru 6 and 10 contained nothing of evidentiary value. All evidence collected was processed and placed into evidence at the Brown County Sheriff's Department. Your affiant tested the green plant stems and the burnt residue in the blunt found in bag 7 using the #8 Duquenois Reagent field test and it showed a positive result for the presence of marijuana in the evidence tested.

Wherefore, the said Deputy Daniel Sandford, a law enforcement officer, prays that a search warrant be issued to search such premises for the said property, and if found, to seize the same and take the property into custody according to law.

_____

Affiant - Law Enforcement Officer

Subscribed and sworn to before me this

3rd day of February 2009.

Honorable _____   Honorable _____

JUDGE OF CIRCUIT COURT BRANCH ___   COURT COMMISSIONER

BROWN COUNTY, WISCONSIN   CIRCUIT COURT BRANCH ___

BROWN COUNTY, WISCONSIN

REFERENCES

American Heritage Dictionary of the English Language. (2017). Retrieved December 15, 2017 from https://ahdictionary.com/

Argiriou, Steven L. (n.d.). "Terry Stop Update: The Law, Field Analysis and Examples." Retrieved December 19, 2017 from https://www.fletc.gov/sites/default/files/imported_files/training/programs/legal-division/downloads-articles-and-faqs/research-by-subject/4th-amendment/terrystopupdate.pdf

Merriam-Webster Dictionary. (2017). Retrieved December 15, 2017 from https://www.merriam-webster.com.

Strunk, William. (1918). *The Elements of Style*. New York: Harcourt, Brace, and Company.

Toadvine, April, Brizee, Allen, and Angeli, Elizabeth. (2017). Active and Passive Voice. Retrieved October 4, 2017 from https://owl.english.purdue.edu/owl/owlprint/539/

Wells, Jaclyn M., and Brizee, Allen. (2017). Writing a Developed and Detailed Conclusion. Retrieved October 4, 2017 from https://owl.english.purdue.edu/engagement/2/2/60/

Wisconsin Department of Justice (WI DOJ). (2014). *Report Writing: A Training Guide for Law Enforcement Officers*. Madison, WI: State of Wisconsin.

INDEX